SIMPLY BRILLIANT

S|MPLY BR|LLIANT

POWERFUL TECHNIQUES TO UNLOCK YOUR CREATIVITY AND Spark NEW IDEAS

BERNHARD SCHROEDER

AMACOM

AMERICAN MANAGEMENT ASSOCIATION

New York • Atlanta • Brussels • Chicago • Mexico City • San Francisco
Shanghai • Tokyo • Toronto • Washington, D.C.

Bulk discounts available. For details visit:
www.amacombooks.org/go/specialsales
Or contact special sales:
Phone: 800-250-5308
Email: specialsls@amanet.org
View all the AMACOM titles at: www.amacombooks.org
American Management Association: www.amanet.org

This publication is designed to provide accurate and authoritative information in regard to the subject matter covered. It is sold with the understanding that the publisher is not engaged in rendering legal, accounting, or other professional service. If legal advice or other expert assistance is required, the services of a competent professional person should be sought.

Library of Congress Cataloging-in-Publication Data

Names: Schroeder, Bernhard, author.
Title: Simply brilliant : powerful techniques to unlock your creativity and
    spark new ideas / by Bernhard Schroeder.
Description: New York, NY : AMACOM, [2016]
Identifiers: LCCN 2016017278| ISBN 9780814437193 (hardcover) | ISBN
    9780814437209 (ebook)
Subjects: LCSH: Creative ability in business. | Creative ability. | Creative
    thinking. | New products.
Classification: LCC HD53 .S37 2016 | DDC 650.1--dc23 LC record available at
    https://lccn.loc.gov/2016017278

About AMA

American Management Association (www.amanet.org) is a world leader in talent development, advancing the skills of individuals to drive business success. Our mission is to support the goals of individuals and organizations through a complete range of products and services, including classroom and virtual seminars, webcasts, webinars, podcasts, conferences, corporate and government solutions, business books, and research. AMA's approach to improving performance combines experiential learning—learning through doing—with opportunities for ongoing professional growth at every step of one's career journey.

Printing number
10 9 8 7 6 5 4 3 2 1

For all the people who were told they were never creative,
this book is for you. Create away.

Here's to the crazy ones, the misfits, the rebels, the troublemakers, the round pegs in the square holes . . . the ones who see things differently—they're not fond of rules. . . . You can quote them, disagree with them, glorify or vilify them, but the only thing you can't do is ignore them because they change things. . . . They push the human race forward, and while some may see them as the crazy ones, we see genius, because the ones who are crazy enough to think that they can change the world are the ones who do.

—STEVE JOBS

CONTENTS

SIMPLY BRILLIANT

WHY CREATIVITY MATTERS IN YOUR CAREER AND LIFE

The chief marketing officer strode into the conference room and sat at the head of a very large conference table—one large enough for me, two of my colleagues, and forty-five of his fellow employees, all directors or vice presidents of product development or marketing. Seven years earlier, the company had been a startup. Their growth had been so meteoric they were now an $8 billion Fortune 500 company with enough executives just in that room to field a basketball league. Nonetheless, they were in trouble.

All eyes turned to the person at the head of the table as he spoke. "As you know, we are under attack from our chief competitor in a very competitive marketplace and we are being engaged in a price war, a place we do not want to be," he said. "In response to that attack, we have hired the most creative marketing agency in the world, and these three senior partners will review our situation and then provide us with a creative marketing response. But more important, they will advise us on innovating our current product offerings so that we can be more competitive." All eyes in the room shifted to us. I could only think of three questions. Who outsources their company's creativity and product innovation to an outside firm? What did all these people actually do? How did they get here?

Today, most people still believe that some of us are born creative and others are not—and that's just the way it is. However, our creativity is not simply inherited, like brown eyes or blonde hair. Most people also still believe that right-brained people are more creative and left-brained people are more analytical, even though research in the past five years has shown that, in fact, we use both sides of our brain when we are being creative. We use both sides of the brain to fire our creative juices.

Many people associate creativity only with artists, writers, designers, and filmmakers, not programmers, for example, or lawyers, marketers, and accountants. But these are exactly the people who imagined online auction marketplaces, simplified legal services and forms, connected people with cars with those needing to be somewhere else, and found an easier way to do accounting for small businesses, creating eBay, LegalZoom, Uber, and Quick-Books, respectively.

The fact is, *everyone is creative,* and you can develop your inherent creative skills just like you would any other skill.

For eighteen years, I worked with big brands and startups as a marketing and branding expert and, with three other partners, built a $1 billion integrated marketing agency with more than 10,000 employees. I worked around "creative" people most of my life, but my belief—and our company's premise—was that everyone in the agency was creative. We never really knew where the brilliant flash of inspiration would come from as we solved customer problems or helped them take advantage of new opportunities. Whether we were introducing new "virtual" automotive technology on the

Mazda website or launching Amazon.com into the marketplace, we saw everything as a challenge that, with a certain amount of focused and structured creativity ("brainstorming"), would ultimately lead to innovative solutions or campaigns. Creativity for us was not a choice. It's what we did every day for our clients and to win new business. Looking back, it seemed chaotically normal. So, if we thought being creative was normal, why doesn't everyone else? Why can't the companies we work in or lead also be creative? As all the research I've done on the subject of creativity and innovation indicates, they can.

Over the past four years, I have taught a course called Creativity and Innovation as part of the Entrepreneurship Program at San Diego State University. Before I taught this particular course, I researched how others taught or introduced creativity into their company culture. That included professors at some of the top universities in the world who sent me their syllabi and leaders at companies like Pixar and Disney, where creativity was high. (Disney has its own head of creativity training.)

And what I learned is that creativity *isn't* something some people have and others don't. We all have it. But we need a growth mindset, one that believes we can learn and grow our intelligence beyond what we were born with. We need to assemble diverse teams of people who "think different" but all agree on the problem at hand and strive to solve it together. To be truly productive, we need to apply brainstorming tools inside of frameworks that use limited time periods and a mentality that a quantity of ideas is initially better than fewer quality ideas. And if we are working inside of a company, senior management has to provide the right culture, environment, and leadership for creativity to thrive. I now know it can work. My own students have shown me their creative abilities year after year, and they continue to amaze me. And yet you may still ask, why is creativity important to you?

According to IBM's 2012 Global Survey of 1,500 CEOs and entrepreneurs, 92 percent indicated that creativity and problem solving was the top trait or skill they look for in hiring or promoting an employee. That's why I ask my students on the first day of class, "Who thinks they are creative?" Unsurprisingly, out of forty-five students, only four to six of them raise their hands. And yet after fifteen weeks of exercises, challenges, hands-on work with new tools, and learning how to spot problems, they've developed a growth mindset that fuels their creative potential. This is the mindset you will gain by reading this book. First, though, we have to address why you're probably reading the book in the first place. Have you, like that tableful of executives from the Fortune 500 company, lost your creativity or never realized you had it?

Consider when you were a young child—let's say between three and six years old. Without even thinking about it, you were naturally creative. Your instinctive curiosity and imagination fueled your day. You drove your parents crazy with the word "why." You created "forts" out of pillows and sofa cushions. You ate dirt to see what it tasted like. You threw food at the wall to see if it would stick. You ate glue to see how it would taste. You got your sister to eat glue to see if she'd become a statue. You created amazing art with just your fingers. You were constantly using your imagination to play make-believe games and create imaginary friends. You had conversations with no one. You were insanely curious. And you were creative.

Research has shown that curiosity is highly linked to creativity, and we (parents, teachers, society, etc.) systematically begin to dull your creativity and ask you to conform between the ages of 4 and 12. Color between the lines. There is always just one right answer. You need to dress appropriately. Then, during your teenage years, your curiosity and potential creativity was further undermined by the premium placed on only the "right answers" for standardized testing. Eventually, little remains of your curious, childlike natural inclination to question and challenge the status quo. You covered your inner well of creativity, maybe without even knowing it.

But creativity and problem solving is exactly the skill most critical to personal, professional, and academic success in today's rapidly changing world. According to education leaders, qualities such as curiosity, creativity, and imagination are for today's kids "what the 'three Rs' were for previous generations." If that's the case, then you'd better understand exactly how creativity and innovation works and how you can get back what you had as a child.

The good news is that you can. You see, it never really left you; it's just hidden. And you need to fire the flames of your "creative" spirit. The only way you will ever achieve your maximum potential is if you become better at solving problems or taking advantage of opportunities. So, let's unleash your creative talent because that's what you need to reap the greatest rewards today and keep ahead of the competition tomorrow.

Forty years ago, businesses assumed that they would have to create new products and services or respond to changes in the marketplace to ensure their viability and success—eventually. Speed was not really rewarded; steady and slow was the norm. Companies would get there when they got there, and customers would just have to wait. Innovation was glacial. It could take years, sometimes decades, before change rippled across global markets. Well, change has changed.

The modern world and marketplaces—global, domestic, and local—are amazingly fast and dynamic; they are now in a constant state of disruption largely thanks to the Internet and large marketplace segments like millennials and baby boomers. The new normal is fast, faster, fastest. All of a sudden, being creative and innovative is a requirement for most companies. That means that the people who are building these companies or working in them need to be more creative. That means *you* need to be more creative or, just like companies that don't innovate, you will be left behind.

WHAT'S IN IT FOR YOU SPECIFICALLY, IN THIS BOOK?

First, you will learn about all the "myths of innovation and creativity"—those things that everyone believes but are not true. Then I will introduce you to my CreativityWorks Framework, which consists of the following: mindset, environment (leadership and culture), habitat, and powerful brainstorming tools. Yes, brainstorming tools. Most brainstorming, as you may have already experienced, is haphazard, hit and miss, and most times a complete waste of time. Using the brainstorming tools I identify, within my recommended structure and time frame, you will begin to yield amazing ideation and creativity that will hopefully lead to innovative solutions. I will walk through the two types of mindset, fixed and growth, and explain why you need to adopt the latter. Then I will introduce you to the steps you can take to heighten individual and team creativity. After that, you will learn how to really set up and conduct brainstorming sessions using six different tools, all in a structured time frame. I will thoroughly walk you through all six different brainstorming tools so that you can understand which one to use when you try to address a problem or take advantage of an opportunity.

If you are not aware of key trends, marketplaces, and disruptions occurring today and emerging in the near future, I will highlight several you should pay attention to—and show you how you can recognize them yourself. Finally, I will share with you the backstories of several entrepreneurs and how they became curious about a problem they encountered, tried to solve it, and ended up creating amazing companies. If you use the knowledge and tools in this book, and adopt a growth mindset, you will become more creative and perhaps you too will create something amazing. All you need to start is to simply reengage your curiosity.

Curiosity is in fact what got me to where I am now. I was born in Europe, but grew up in New York and Michigan, one of five children. I had a pretty normal childhood, but I questioned everything, which got me into some trouble both at school and with my parents. I can't really tell you why; I was not trying to be a rebel. I was just curious about how and why things worked. I did not really believe everything that people told me—I had to see, taste, or explore it for myself. Right when I was graduating college in 1983, I had two job offers; one salary was fully twice as much as the other. But I was curious about a marketing agency that said it was using computers to drive marketing. I knew nothing about computers and little about marketing but felt, based on my curiosity and instinct, they were critical to my future. So I chose the lesser paying job. That curiosity paid off very well as I got in at the beginning of database marketing and working at the agency hastened the development of my marketing knowledge and skills. Within one year, the agency asked for volunteers to launch a spinoff business that would focus on customer satisfaction and customer loyalty programs. I joined the team. I'd bet well; the spinoff exploded to $20 million in revenue in two years (about $50 million in 2016 dollars), as did my responsibilities and career. In the next few years, I further developed my marketing expertise and fed my curiosity about the future by learning how to recognize and follow trends. I read voraciously and networked with industry thought leaders and analysts. I wanted to understand the potential future before it got here. If I could do that, my clients would value me immensely. I challenged myself to know more than the next person. I also challenged myself to find other people like me so that we could build an amazing company. I didn't know where they were exactly, but I knew they were not in Detroit, so I accepted an opportunity to work with clients in New York.

Later, while in New York working on the Mercedes-Benz account, I was flying first class to San Francisco on business and I sat next to a person about seven years younger than me. I was in a dark blue Brooks Brothers suit and he was dressed in blue jeans and a polo shirt. I was curious why this person sitting in first class was dressed, well, rather casually. Turned out he was the director of marketing for a company called Apple Computer. We had an amazing four-hour conversation. I marketed cars that came out once a year; he sold new computer products *every* quarter. I was so curious about the challenge of marketing new products every quarter, and this young executive, with only a couple years of experience, was so fearlessly creative. I instinctively knew the people I was looking for were in California. Within one year, I had moved to Silicon Valley and was working with Apple on several marketing programs.

One day the senior VP of marketing at Apple suggested that I meet the founders of a small graphic design agency. Initially, I was not interested. He suggested it again about two weeks later, telling me that the founders were some of the most creative marketing people he had ever met. Now, I was curious. I met with them for one hour, walked outside, leaned against the wall, and knew that I had just found the most creative people I had ever met, too. One person was a former creative director at Apple; the other two had strategic marketing experience in consumer foods and technology. They were all about thirty-two years old. Within one year, I joined them, and in the next seven years we built the best integrated marketing agency in the world, which we would take through an initial public offering (IPO) and grow to over 10,000 employees, with $1.2 billion in annual revenue and offices in thirty countries. Best creative years of my life.

Later, after eight years as a turnaround executive, I found my way to San Diego State University. I was curious about whether I had what it takes to teach young minds. Shortly after beginning my career at SDSU, I met a man at a university networking event. We ended up sitting next to each other, and after we politely said hello to each other, I noticed that he seemed stressed out. So I asked him how his day was going. He was the executive director of the entrepreneurship center and he lamented that he was losing a key person. I told him about my background and he asked why I was wasting my time just teaching two courses. He suggested I join the center and work with him in running the current programs. I told him his current strategy and programs regarding the center sounded "terminally disinteresting." He asked for forty-eight hours to put together three strategic objectives that he felt would challenge me in a way that would also greatly benefit the university. When we met again, the three strategic objectives were so large that initially I did not think I could accomplish them in anything less than five years. He had piqued my curiosity. Within thirty days, I was the director of the entrepreneurship center at SDSU, where today I still run the center's programs and teach in the entrepreneurship program. Today, San Diego State University is ranked in the top twenty entrepreneurship programs in the United States, according to *Forbes* and *U.S. News & World Report*.

Curiosity had taken me a long way and still does today. I wrote a book called *Fail Fast or Win Big* that was published in 2015, all because I agreed to do a TEDx talk. My editor, who was curious about TEDx talks he could turn into books, found my talk through an acquaintance and contacted me. We had several conversations over a five-week time period and I signed a contract to write *Fail Fast or Win Big*. *Simply Brilliant* came about because I was curious about teaching a course on creativity and innovation in the entrepreneurship program. The more I researched, the more I wanted to teach this kind of a course. It just so happened that the department chair was looking for someone else to teach the class. I agreed to teach the class if I could have one year to do the research and to design the course. He agreed, and I have taught the class for four years now to what I hope are insanely curious students. When I told my editor about wanting to write a book based on the class, he, being curious himself, said, "Go for it."

For most of my career, my practical experience has centered on creative people and the innovative solutions we crafted. We had what David and Tom Kelley from IDEO like to call "creative confidence." We had a growth mindset that overcame any personal mental blocks or misgivings about being creative. We believed we were creative and were supposed to come up with innovative solutions, so we did. You can too. You just need to believe that you are creative. My mission today, at San Diego State University, in the San Diego community, and with this book, is to help as many people like yourself to realize you have the potential to be amazingly creative.

I will invite you to begin your creativity journey with this quote from one of my former students who took my Creativity and Innovation course. It illustrates why I teach this course:

Ever since I can remember, everyone has told me that I am not creative. My parents told me, my teachers told me, and my friends even remarked that I was just not creative. However, after taking this course, I am shocked to learn that I am creative. Our teams came up with great solutions to the problems we faced in our group projects. And I often found myself being the one who suggested ideas that led to a breakthrough in our projects. With the knowledge I have gleaned from this course, the books we read about the myths of innovation, and the creative exercises and tools we learned to use, I am going to live the rest of my life knowing that I am creative and can lead teams to be creative and perhaps even innovative. Thanks for changing my life.

What have people told you your entire life? Do you feel creative? Do you really want to be more creative? If so, read on.

1

THE MYTHS OF CREATIVITY AND INNOVATION

Myths are fascinating. If you believe a myth just enough, it becomes a "truth." But in reality, it is still a myth. To better understand the "myths" surrounding creativity and innovation, let's draw perspective and insight from someone whom you might not put on your short list of creative people. But he was. Albert Einstein. To hear Einstein talk about himself, he was not a creative genius; he just believed in himself and felt he worked harder than others to solve problems. He had three things to say about himself:

Follow your curiosity: *"I have no special talent. I am only passionately curious."* Curiosity helps to fuel our imagination. When we ask questions of others, we can find out important information to help us solve problems, open new doors, and form connections. When we ask questions of ourselves, we can shake up our beliefs, reveal our innermost desires, and make positive change. Curiosity becomes the alchemy for innovation.

It's worth pointing out that you don't necessarily have to have existing problems you want to solve, doors you want to open, or connections you want to make right now. Being curious all the time discovers and saves up all the ingredients for when you do have to perform some alchemy later.

Imagination is powerful: *"Imagination is everything. It is the preview of life's coming attractions. Imagination is more important than knowledge."* With one idea, an empire can be built. Take, for example, Walt Disney, a true master of imagination. He built an empire on the back of a mouse. When Universal Pictures took his original animation character, a rabbit named Oswald, he was stunned. Faced with what he felt was betrayal, he and his Disney Brothers Studio worked even harder and readapted the rabbit character into a mouse called Mickey. While not initially successful, within six months he produced the first animated movie with music and sound effects and it was an instant hit. Imagination and creativity opened the doors of possibilities; today Disney/Pixar is the leading animation company in the world.

Perseverance is priceless: *"It's not that I'm so smart; it's just that I stay with problems longer."* If you have a goal at work or in your life, you'll be faced with obstacles, but by staying with problems longer, as Einstein says, it can mean the difference between failure and success. Another amazingly creative inventor, Thomas Edison, said it perfectly. "I have not failed. I've just found 10,000 ways that won't work." I have seen and worked with countless entrepreneurs who ultimately persevere not so much because of their intelligence or luck, but because they outwork everyone else.

As simple as Einstein makes things—after all, he reduced the complex relationship of matter and light to energy in the most elegant and famous equation in physics—the first step is to not limit yourself into believing you are *not* creative. That means not believing these longstanding myths.

THE MYTHS OF CREATIVITY

Creativity is something that everyone has inside of them. And yet the common belief in our society is that some people are just born creative and the rest of us are not. Nothing could be further from the truth. Let's examine some of the common creativity myths.

The Flash of Insight

New ideas sometimes seem to appear as a flash of insight. But research shows that such insights are actually the culmination of working on the problem for a period of time. Everyone remembers the Wright brothers' first successful flight, just not the previous three years of experiments and failures. We remember what worked and what did not work, and we build on it. This thinking is then given time to incubate in the subconscious mind as we connect threads before the ideas emerge as new "just thought of it" innovations. As Steve Jobs put it:

Creativity is just connecting things. When you ask creative people how they did something, they feel a little guilty because they didn't really do it—they just saw something. It seemed obvious to them after a while. That's because they were able to connect experiences they've had and synthesize new things.

The Creativity Gene

Many people believe that creative ability is a trait inherent in one's DNA or genes. That, in fact, if your parents or relatives were creative artists or designers, then you will be creative. But the evidence does not support this belief. In 2009, researchers published a study in *Harvard Business Review* where they concluded that creativity is 20 percent inherited and 80 percent learned behavior. People who have confidence in themselves and work the hardest on a problem are the ones most likely to come up with a creative or innovative solution. Would you necessarily get a creative person from parents who were an attorney and nonprofit evangelist? What if all he did was program computers? Yet, was Bill Gates, Microsoft's cofounder, creative? You bet.

The Original Idea

According to Ecclesiastes, which dates to the third century BC, there was already "nothing new under the sun." While some intellectual property (IP) attorneys might argue that that's not true and that a person can own a creative idea, history and empirical research show more evidence that new ideas are actually combinations of older ideas and that sharing those ideas helps generate more innovation. "Innovation and Iteration: Friends Not Foes," written by Scott Anthony for the *Harvard Business Review* (May 12, 2008), illustrates this point exactly. He showcases several new product examples in Silicon Valley that were derivatives of other iterations before they achieved a level of innovation. We needed to develop a flip phone, then a smartphone, to come up with a smartwatch.

"If I have seen further, it is by standing on the shoulders of giants," Isaac Newton wrote to fellow scientist Robert Hooke, echoing, appropriately, an idea first expressed four centuries earlier.

Ed Catmull, president of Pixar, talks about how critical "the creative team" is to the growth of an idea that forms an amazing film. To paraphrase him, no one might remember who offered up the single idea for a rat that could be a chef, but *Ratatouille* became a great movie due to thousands of additional ideas from an amazingly creative team. So, share and spark as many ideas as you can and see where it goes. Don't worry about trying to come up with something brand new. Instead, create something amazing.

The Innovation Expert

Many companies today still rely on a technical expert or team of experts to generate a stream of creative ideas. Naturally, the experts will fulfill that expectation by providing answers based on their past experience. Therein lies the problem. People with the most in-depth knowledge and experience typically prefer the methods that have made them successful in the past and dismiss new approaches they have not tried before. Instead, research suggests that particularly tough problems often require the diverse perspectives of an outsider or someone not limited by the knowledge of why something can't be done. So-called beginner's mind refers to the propensity to approach each situation with openness and few preconceptions, no matter how many times you've encountered it before. Tom and David Kelley make this very clear in their book *Creative Confidence*, which is based on the principles of their creative consultancy firm, IDEO.

Rewards Drive Creativity

The expert myth often leads to another myth, which argues that larger incentives, monetary or otherwise, will increase motivation and therefore increase innovation. Incentives can help, but often they do more harm than good, as people learn to game the system. In *Drive*, Daniel Pink highlights the rather stunning amount of counterintuitive research that suggests that money can actually make people *less motivated* to do creative work. That is, once people have a base level of money that makes them comfortable, using monetary incentives to get them to do creative work not only fails, but leads to worse performance. Creativity and innovation, it's been shown, are their own reward.

The Lone Inventor

Just as the great men of history weren't the only ones to make history, the great innovators didn't create their works alone. Most people, for instance, believe Steve Jobs created Apple. I liked Steve Jobs. Our marketing agency worked with him at NeXT, Pixar, and Apple. But there was a core team that really helped start and accelerate Apple. Steve Wozniak and Mike Markkula were incredibly important. Wozniak was the technology expert and Markkula supplied the marketing and sales expertise. Creativity is a team effort, and recent research into how to incorporate creativity in a company's culture can help leaders or entrepreneurs assemble amazing teams.

The Prerequisite Brainstorm

Many company managers today preach the use of brainstorming as a way to spark creative ideas that might yield innovative products or services. Unfortunately, very few of the "corporate" brainstorming sessions I have ever attended yielded anything but the frustration of wasted time. The real genius of brainstorming isn't the number of ideas listed in a short period of time. Instead, it's the many various combinations of ideas that can develop when individuals share their own thoughts with each other. Those combinations could never occur apart from interaction. To make brainstorming really effective, use a brainstorm tool, a time-based framework, and clear rules. And try to generate as many "conversations" and ideas as possible. In the early moments of brainstorming, the quantity of ideas always trumps quality.

The Happy Company

Believers in this myth want everyone to get along, believing that this "happy" environment might foster innovation. That's why we see so many "creative" companies build workplaces where employees play foosball and enjoy free lunches together. But breakthroughs leading to innovation come from creative dissent. In fact, many of the most creative companies have found ways to structure dissent and conflict into their environment to better push their employees' creative limits and to question what is possible without any regard to past and present solutions. You have to embrace that the world is changing and that you need to adapt, create, and innovate. That kind of thinking would have helped Borders bookstores and Blockbuster.

More Resources = More Creativity

Another popular notion is that constraints hinder our creativity and the most innovative results come from people who have "unlimited" resources. Research shows, however, that creativity loves constraints. In our own agency, we did the best work when we had limited time and client resources. You had to be more creative just to make everything work harder. I have often said our marketing teams were more creative on $5 million accounts than $100 million accounts. Today, when working with startups, I am amazed at the creativity you have to have when you only have $25,000. Perhaps companies should do just the opposite—intentionally apply limits to leverage the creative potential of their people.

If you believe your company's or startup's success depends on your being more creative than your competitors, don't just blindly follow these creativity myths. Instead spend the time needed to understand and nurture the components of creativity in your environment. How creatively are you or your company pursuing innovation? Or are the myths of creativity holding you back? At the same time, don't fall prey to these innovation myths.

THE MYTHS OF INNOVATION

I honestly don't know if most people could actually explain or define the "process" of innovation. Can innovation be predicted? Can you innovate on purpose or on demand? I don't think so. And yet innovation occurs every day. That means that quite a few people out there either don't know or care about any myths of innovation. So, let's examine and debunk the top ones.

We Know History

So much of what we think we know comes from our knowledge of history about anything. But do we know the real history of any major innovation? Writers and historians tend to shape history as if it were a creative story: chronological, precise, with characters overcoming conflicts and their own limitations. The problem with that is it puts us into a limited and defined area. We then believe in something so strongly related to the history of that innovation that we may actually not examine the real failures, which led to the innovation. For any major innovation you may know in your industry, examine its real history.

The Innovation Formula

The challenge with being innovative, especially in a given market-place, is the many factors that are beyond your control. You can do everything right and still fail. Industry analysts and technology leaders would have us believe they can see the future of innovations that they believe will actually occur. Is there an innovation formula? Really, that's impossible. Innovation is not predictable. It's like understanding Moore's Law (which says the power of computing doubles every two years) and somehow knowing what technology device to manufacture that consumers will love. While innovation will never cease, you can't really use a methodology or formula to innovate. You just keep iterating or improving current ideas until you create or stumble to a breakthrough.

New Ideas Are the Best

As humans, in general, we are pretty conservative and don't embrace new ideas easily. Don't believe me? The next time you are in a meeting, sing your answers to questions. How accepting would your peers be? Conformity is deep in our biology. While talking about creativity is very popular, actually being creative scares people. The thing we need to understand is that most great ideas were rejected, often for years or decades. You may remember the debacle that followed when Coca-Cola tried to introduce "New Coke" and customers howled until the company removed it from the marketplace. Or that we needed illegal music download companies like Napster for the entertainment industry to begin embracing digital music. The history of innovation is a tale of persistence against rejection. The likelihood is that no one will initially like your creative idea. So, remember to be persistent.

Great Ideas Are Rare

If you think it's hard to come up with lots of new ideas, just go to a kindergarten class when they are creating something. They will invent dozens of things in an hour. In less than forty minutes, students in my Creativity and Innovation class at SDSU will create fourteen new products that solve a real problem. The truth is humans were designed to be creative. The problem is the societal norm of adult life demands conformity, and so we sacrifice our creative instincts in favor of accepted social status. Think back to your elementary or high school class when you raised your hand and provided what you thought was a pretty creative answer to a problem. And the class laughed and the teacher said your idea was not possible. How long was it before you raised your hand again in that class? Good ideas are everywhere; the tough part is getting people to believe and then act on them.

My Manager Knows More Than Me

Many people believe that their senior managers are better at everything than they are. Because this thinking is wrong in so many ways, creativity takes a real beating. To rise in a company demands hard work and good political judgment, yet innovation requires a willingness to defy convention and take a risk. Risk takers are harder to promote in most organizations, yet essential for progress. To blindly assume your senior management leadership is the best at leading innovation is a mistake. It sure did not help BlackBerry. Here is a quote from the company's then founder and CEO: "How much presence does Apple have in business? It's vanishingly small," Mike Lazaridis said in an interview with the *Guardian* newspaper when Apple revealed the iPhone in 2007. Enough said.

The Best Idea Wins

It's tough to admit but the best ideas don't always win. Why? We love the "myth" of the winner. Edison invents the lightbulb? Not really, as he lost a patent lawsuit to a person named Joseph Swan. The Europeans invented the firearm? Not really. The Japanese did years earlier, but their culture embraced the symbol of the sword. Betamax videotape was far superior to VHS and so it would succeed as the best idea, right? No, VHS was poorer in quality but the tape format was three times longer and that's what consumers preferred. In the 1930s, major cities in the United States had public transportation—trolleys and tram systems modeled on successful designs from Europe. So you would expect we would further innovate on that success and build the world's best public transportation systems? Not really. Turns out we liked cars. The best idea does not always win. If you have a great idea, fight for it.

Solutions Are More Exciting Than Problems

Einstein said, "If I had twenty days to solve a problem I would take nineteen to define it." There are many creative ways to think about a problem, and different ways to look at a potential solution. However, we are impatient, and so we love to quickly look at potential solutions when trying to solve a problem. The problem with that approach is that we tend to overlook what we no longer see. If you really want to be creative and perhaps even innovative, take your time and really define or agree on the real problem. That is the most critical thing you can do before embarking on the solution mission.

There is just one more myth to debunk: the one that says your potential creativity is determined by whether you have a dominant left or right brain.

Right Brain vs. Left Brain

From self-help and business success books to job applications and smartphone apps, the theory that the different halves of the human brain govern different skills and personality traits is a popular one. No doubt at some point in your life you've been schooled on "left-brained" and "right-brained" thinking—that people who use the right side of their brains are more creative, spontaneous, and subjective while those who tap the left side are more logical, detail oriented, and analytical. Too bad it's not true. However, since so many people believe this myth, it becomes a self-fulfilling prophecy. If we are told at a young age we are creative, we lean in and try to become an artist or designer. Even if we are really not that creative, we work harder, believing success is right around the corner. If we are told we are not creative, we then focus on less creative opportunities, thinking we will never succeed in a "creative" profession. Well, this "myth" has existed for hundreds of years, but newer research studies and scientific experiments dispute it.

The brain isn't as clear-cut as the myth makes it out to be. For example, the right hemisphere is involved in processing some aspects of language, such as intonation and emphasis. In one such study done in 2012, University of Utah neuroscientists scanned the brains of more than 1,000 people, ages 7 to 29, while they were lying quietly or reading, measuring their functional lateralization—the specific mental processes taking place on each side of the brain. They segmented the brain into 7,000 regions, and while they did uncover patterns for why a brain connection might be strongly left- or right-lateralized, they found no evidence that the study participants had a stronger left- or right-sided brain network.

How, then, did the left-brained/right-brained theory take root? Experts suggest the myth dates back to the 1800s, when scientists discovered that an injury to one side of the brain caused a loss of specific cognitive abilities. The concept gained ground in the 1960s with the Nobel Prize–winning "split brain" work of neuropsychologists Roger Sperry and Michael Gazzaniga. The researchers conducted studies with patients who had undergone surgery to cut the corpus callosum—the band of neural fibers that connect the hemispheres—as a last-resort treatment for epilepsy. They discovered that when the two sides of the brain weren't able to communicate with each other, they responded differently to stimuli, indicating that the hemispheres have different functions.

But the research was limited and drew no real conclusions. However, psychologists picked up on this research and continued to promote the myth of right-brain versus left-brain creativity over the next thirty years. Pretty soon we had personality and job occupation tests that, based on the results, told us what we were potentially good at concerning a job or career. How insane. How many of us remember that disruptive, super funny, or creative student who was "counseled" by schoolteachers to go to an automotive or IT school instead of college? Heck, that person probably could write a show like *Breaking Bad*. Oh, he did. Vince Gilligan, the creator of the hit show *Breaking Bad*, grew up with parents who were a schoolteacher and insurance claims adjuster in Richmond,

Virginia. But his best friend's mother lent him a film camera and encouraged him to shoot films and enter them in local competitions. Turns out he was pretty good.

Okay, here's the truth. As research has proved, we use both sides of our brains to do both creative and analytical thinking or tasks. So, you are not technically left- or right-brained. You can be as creative as you want to be. Just adopt the right mindset and exercise your "creative muscles" regularly.

THE CREATIVITYWORKS FRAMEWORK

I spent my entire career having to be creative and leading teams to come up with some innovative solutions. Without even knowing it, I was essentially using the core elements of a creativity framework that I use today in my Creativity and Innovation course at San Diego State University. I looked at the common themes in creative people and companies. What I discovered was what led me to create the CreativityWorks Framework and its key components of mindset, environment, habitat, and brainstorming tools. Let me explain each briefly before going into more depth on each one in the following chapters.

Mindset: To be creative, you have to consciously believe you are creative. You have to have a growth mindset, one that is in a continual state of learning or acquiring more knowledge and open to new ideas.

Environment: I define environment as having two key attributes in my creativity framework: leadership and culture. Think about your current work environment or one in the past. Was the leadership open to new ideas? Did the company's leaders embrace creativity and innovation? Related to leadership, what is or was your work environment culture? Were ideas shared openly? Was there a formal hierarchy or did the best idea win? You cannot have creativity unless you have a great environment.

Habitat: I define habitat as the physical customer or employee workspace. For example, our marketing agency offices were open, colorful, and free-flowing. You felt creative just walking into one of our offices. If you feel creative, you are more likely to be creative. Google offices are an amazing cornucopia of color and imagination at work with cocoon pods for small meetings and slides that connect floors. Pixar allows employees to decorate their office spaces and model them after their favorite movie or character. Pretty cool, right? No, pretty creative.

Brainstorming Tools: Brainstorming without using a given framework or tool is a waste of time. I will introduce you to some amazing brainstorming structures and tools in upcoming chapters and suggest a brainstorm format.

If using a framework is intended to have you be more creative, how do you define the difference between creativity and innovation? One of the key definitions we use in class is that creativity is the generation of ideas to a potential problem while innovation is the actual implementation of a new idea to solve a problem. It's incredible to me that by using this framework in my class, students can come up with an amazing array of creative ideas and potential solutions. In one class exercise led by a former IDEO employee, the creative solution to a problem presented by a student team was so potentially innovative, the guest lecturer leaned over to me and quietly said, "That's a multimillion-dollar solution if implemented."

CREATIVELY DEFINING THE PROBLEM

As a director in the Lavin Entrepreneurship Center at San Diego State University, I meet quite a few company CEOs/founders, startup entrepreneurs, and student wannabe entrepreneurs. When these student entrepreneurs meet me to pitch their idea, I often stop them before they get started and simply say this: "What problem are you solving?" If they say "Huh?" then I know we have yards to go. That's okay. After all, I am on a college campus and the acquisition of knowledge is at our core purpose. I sit down with them and ask how much due diligence they have done to accurately analyze and define the problem. I might ask the following questions:

- What have you done to clearly clarify and identify the problem? How many "why" or "why else" questions have you asked?
- How exactly have you researched the problem? Have you talked to any customers?
- Have you framed a creative challenge around the words "How could I . . ." without using evaluation criteria?
- Based on an understanding of the problem, how many ideas have you created that could potentially solve the problem? Did you hold a brainstorming session?
- How did you evaluate your best ideas? Have you thought about combining any of your ideas to solve the problem?
- Do you have an action plan with simple steps to test your best idea?
- Have you tested your idea? What is the least costly and least risky way of testing your idea?

I like to really emphasize to these future entrepreneurs how critical it is to correctly identify the problem before you start throwing solutions around like confetti. Identifying the problem is also a core mantra of my Creativity and Innovation course. We spend an inordinate amount of time in my class discussing and agreeing on the problem before we begin any creative brainstorming exercise that involves generating solutions.

I will end this chapter with this quote.

> The key question isn't "What fosters creativity?" But it is why in God's name isn't everyone creative? Where was the human potential lost? How was it crippled? I think therefore a good question might be not why do people create? But why do people not create or innovate? We have got to abandon that sense of amazement in the face of creativity, as if it were a miracle if anybody created anything.
>
> **—ABRAHAM MASLOW**

CREATIVE / INNOVATIVE INSIGHT

When I was leading a team on the Mazda account, the VP of marketing was so impressed with our team's ability to be creative and get things done that she introduced me to an executive at Ford who was looking for insights into how technology and communications would meet in the car. He asked if I had any ideas. I told him I did not but that we had very creative people who could examine that problem and come up with a potential solution. He asked if we could come up with a solution to demonstrate to top Ford executives in ninety days. Crazy

(continued on next page)

(continued from previous page)

deadline. My response, "Send me a Lincoln dashboard." I assembled a very diverse team, none of whom had previous automotive experience; we met several times, once to define the problem and then several times to brainstorm ideas. We came up with a "day in the life" of a Ford owner scenario. For the demo, we actually placed a small screen in the dashboard. We used touchscreen technology, in combination with video, all done in multimedia software. The demo went like this: As the owner walked out to his car in the morning, the car door unlocked as it sensed his presence. When he started the car, it said, "Hi." Then, on the touchscreen, it showed traffic and route optimization options. Then the car asked if he would like to have his email read to him. We demoed speech-to-text technology and owner video on demand. And so on and so on.

Our team of designers, writers, programmers, strategists, and one intern created an amazing "futurist" solution. We made the presentation to top Ford executives in a private conference room in a nondescript building in Dearborn, Michigan. The demonstration went flawlessly. We never heard from Ford again about the project. The year was 1998.

Key Takeaway

If you are building your career, embrace the idea that you need to be more creative in order to solve problems and be innovative. If you are a manager, give people the right culture and environment and encourage creativity in whatever they do. Together, you might just build an innovative company.

CHAPTER TWO

THE CREATIVITYWORKS FRAMEWORK

Please pick up the nearest pen, any pen will do, and ask yourself, "How could I create a new pen that will meet my needs in the next five years?" Take a few moments. Draw what your new pen would look like. How far did you push the device beyond what a moment ago you considered just any pen?

On the second meeting of my class during the semester, I ask the same of my students. I walk in, set a pen on my desk, and say, "This pen no longer meets my needs. Get into groups of four people each and create a new pen for me, one that has multiple functionalities and will meet my needs in the next five years." Initially, the students just stare at me, this being only our second class. Then I bark, "You are in a Creativity and Innovation course. Get into groups and use the CreativityWorks Framework to design me a new pen in the next forty minutes. Go."

Now the pace of the students is frenetic before they settle into a quiet buzz as they work their way through the challenge using one of the brainstorming tools introduced in the first class (and that you, too, will learn about later). The pace picks up again forty minutes later when they present their drawings for an amazing new pen. Some of the features suggested include a USB drive, automatic note-taking transfer to my laptop, an emergency LED light, Bluetooth locator, text messaging display from a smartphone, and for women, a small lipstick applicator. And there are many more creative ideas. It's only the second class of the semester but the students now understand; they own the creativity in this class. Before I walk you through the CreativityWorks Framework, let's review what you need to own.

CREATIVITY STARTS WITH YOU

I am always amazed when I meet with company executives or founders of startups and they have no idea that "employee creativity" starts with each employee. I don't care what type of company or industry you are in—a law firm, restaurant, accounting, banking, or a mobile applications company—you "own" the creativity that happens in the organization. Are you telling me that people at law firms and banks don't need to be creative in either introducing new products or solving problems? Are you going to leave creativity and innovation in your company to chance? You get to choose creativity. Here are some simple ways to "jumpstart" your own creativity mindset:

▲ **Open your eyes.** Do you really see what is going on in your company, in the marketplace, and with worldwide trends (i.e., organic foods, renting via Uber and Airbnb, mobile banking and transactions, etc.) that affects you or your customers?

▲ **Make new mind connections.** When was the last time you read a book not related to your business or attended a trade show or event that had nothing to do with your industry? Pick up new knowledge or, better yet, a new skill.

▲ **Talk to your customer.** When was the last time you had a conversation with a real customer? How many customers do you talk to regularly to get their insights or to develop a little customer empathy?

▲ **Really observe something.** Do you take note of colors, smells, and sounds that make up a brand or retail presence? When was the last time you took a different route to work or walked into a store you have never been in before?

▲ **Ask "why" more.** As you meet with people and look to help them solve problems, do you form your own opinions quickly and ask eighty-word questions, likely to confirm those opinions, or do you simply ask "why" more often, then just listen? For example, pretend you run a ketchup company. Your VP of sales says, "Sales are down." You ask, "Why?" "We ran out of inventory." "Why?" "We had problems related to the new product." "Why?" "There was a shortage of a key component." "Why?" "We only have one supplier." Aha! Now you know the real problem, and it's not that sales of ketchup are down.

▲ **Reframe your challenge.** Instead of looking at a challenge from one "closed" perspective, step back and reframe it. For example, your VP of sales is back to say again, "Sales are down." "Why?" "We don't know why, so let's run a promotion to move more ketchup." "What if we lower the price?" "That will hurt gross margins, net profits, and our brand." And you're stuck. What if you changed your old way of doing things, though—in this case by expanding your product line to include mustard, using your same manufacturing and distribution channels? What if you reconceived of your business as not a ketchup company but as a condiment company? In fact, in April 2015 this is precisely what Heinz did, entering the $400 million retail consumer mustard marketplace. That's how you reframe a sales challenge.

▲ **Build your creative network.** Who do you hang out with both at work and in your personal life? How many "creative" people are in your network? When was the last time you had a "creative" conversation with someone not in your profession?

CREATIVITY: FOCUS ON SOLVING PROBLEMS

You have an amazing idea, and it's a big one. You're super motivated. You're blindly passionate. You're pretty smart. So here is the question: Is a good idea really all it takes to build a great business? A great idea, that's what it's all about, right? Wrong. When I first meet with entrepreneurs or company leaders, I don't want to hear their idea about the products being built or services provided. First and foremost, I want to hear about problems—those that exist and those that can be solved. Quite a few people, particularly first-time entrepreneurs or product developers, kind of want to scratch their own itch. They have a vision for a product and they want to see it in the marketplace. They are the worst kind of customer. They are their own customer.

As long as consumers have problems, they will forever be on the hunt for solutions. People will always look for better, faster, and smarter ways to accomplish everyday tasks. And fortunately for entrepreneurs and marketers, there's still lots of room for improvement in existing products. That said, the biggest issue for most people is finding these painful problems and matching them with the best solutions possible.

So focus on building a *must-have* product, not a nice-to-have one. Consumers are overwhelmed with the paradox of choice on a daily basis. Attention spans are getting shorter in the age of multitasking and only a few products are getting noticed—with many being a solution for a want and not a need. The demand for quicker and faster results (i.e., lose weight now, play a mobile game now, listen to music now, get somewhere now, etc.) makes it very difficult to fully satisfy the needs of consumers. You need to be doing something different and better to make it in this world, as consumers expect and demand more than just another product. So, what do you do?

Solve really painful problems. Google made search better. Amazon simplified online buying and selling. Netflix solved on-demand streaming media. Uber is making on-demand car service better. Airbnb is making travel accommodations more flexible. What can you make smarter or better? What problem can you solve? What do customers need? What is the one painful problem your potential customers (and, hopefully, they comprise a big marketplace) have that you can solve without a struggle? If you come up with a product that is not a must-have, you could still find a way to repurpose it to solve a pressing need. If you have been able to identify a crucial problem that you can effectively execute and deliver to market, you will be able to create a real product or business that matters.

Now how does an entrepreneur or corporate manager go about figuring out which problems to tackle? Well, if you have industry expertise or experience you have an advantage in creating solutions to issues you've dealt with firsthand. But for hopeful founders or product developers who may not have experience in a given space, there are other ways to come up with the next great idea. You've just got to start talking to people. The more you do, the more you'll start to see patterns. The more patterns you see, the more likely you can uncover a problem.

A person with a creative mindset looks at a problem and knows it's an opportunity. That's not a cliché. A problem is literally an opportunity to get paid if you can be the one to solve it. Successful people make their living identifying problems and then providing those solutions to the marketplace. Every good product solves some sort of problem. Even video or app-based games solve a problem—they provide a way for people to unwind after a stressful day and fulfill a fantasy.

If you want to be successful, your natural response to any given problem should always be to ask yourself how you can solve that problem. Not who is to blame, and not how that problem came to be—just how the problem can be solved. Problem solving should become a habit. As you become alert to problems with no solutions, you become alert to new ways to create, grow, develop, and innovate new products. If you can marry your new "alertness" to calculated action, you will develop the instincts that you need to potentially implement innovative solutions that solve problems so well, you will create an amazing new product or company.

Of course, it's not easy to start an innovative new company. According to a report by the Kaufman Foundation, a research center that studies entrepreneurship, roughly 2 million new businesses are started each year. We also know about 90 percent of startups ultimately fail—many, I suspect, because they should never have been started. The company didn't have the right idea; it didn't know the right market or it wasn't the right time for the idea, yet the founders plunged ahead anyway. I am not saying that entrepreneurs or company leaders cannot adjust or pivot their business model, but quite of few of them simply don't know when or how to pivot the business idea they are in love with.

Creating the spark for new ideas that can lead to new companies is, however, much easier, especially if you follow the Creativity-Works Framework.

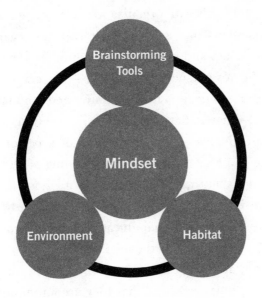

[THE CREATIVITYWORKS FRAMEWORK]

Let me pick up where I left off in Chapter 1 and expand some more on the framework's four components in this chapter and then go into more depth on each in the subsequent chapters.

1. **A Growth Mindset:** The most critical component of the framework, a growth mindset, is also the one you control

completely. Having this mindset is not just a question of having a positive attitude; it's an outlook or internal belief that you are, can be, and will be creative. It is deeply personal, and it informs how you interact with your creativity from everyday work-related ideas to life-changing projects or goals. How you think and feel about creativity guides your life, and it empowers your professional success, your personal purpose, and your creative lifestyle.

2. **Environment:** Environment encapsulates the *culture and leadership* within an organization, whether it's a Fortune 500 company or a startup. Culture is an organization's shared values and beliefs. "Leadership," as Peter Drucker says, "is not magnetic personality—that can just as well be a glib tongue. It is not 'making friends and influencing people'—that is flattery. Leadership is lifting a person's vision to higher sights, the raising of a person's performance to a higher standard, the building of a personality beyond its normal limitations." With good leadership, culture isn't forced; it is fluid and constantly evolving in a positive way. Communication is open and frequent. Everyone understands the mission and goals of the organization, and everyone has input into how they can be attained. Employees feel that they are an important part of the company and that every job matters and everyone is respected within the company. Trust flows up and down the org chart, and everyone is focused on customers.

3. **Habitat:** You can't really maximize the creativity in yourself unless you are in a physical space that promotes both the "creative feeling" and interactivity with other people. Creative spaces designed to promote these activities increase the likelihood of collisions—and the data repeatedly demonstrates that the more "employee" collisions

you can create in a physical space, the more you create positive outcomes. We don't measure the content of inter- actions, but that doesn't matter. When collisions occur, regardless of their content, improvement typically fol- lows. As the *Harvard Business Review* noted in an article on Pixar, Steve Jobs believed physical space mattered. He was adamant that restrooms, cafeterias, and meeting rooms be in central locations to increase the interaction "collisions" between designers, writers, animators, and production people. Of course, Pixar's leaders embrace diverse and open teams, cross-collaboration, and open- ness to feedback; this company culture creates a sense of purpose that permeates the campus. Pixar's habitat, though, is what enables leadership and culture to become manifested as wonderful movies.

4. **Brainstorming Tools:** Based on my twenty years of working with both large corporations and startup companies, my research, and the course I teach, I have come to the conclu- sion that most brainstorming is ineffective because it does not start with a clearly defined problem, an alignment of the solutions objectives (as related to the problem), and a structured format with clear time limits. Well-designed brainstorming, however, can be very effective. In later chapters, I will explain six powerful brainstorming tools in detail (SCAMPER, IdeaGen, Phoenix List, Blue Ocean Strategy, Tempero, and Observation Lab) to help you focus your creativity and generate potential ideas and avoid having your brainstorming session degenerate into a free- for-all of pointless ideas.

The CreativityWorks Framework can be a powerful men- tality and process for you to use in your pursuit of creativity and innovation. But remember, the most important element in creativity and innovation is still the customer.

CUSTOMER TRUTH CAN DRIVE INNOVATION

In my book *Fail Fast or Win Big*, I dedicated an entire chapter to what I call customer truth. I used the adage that "customers are not always right but they are never wrong." In other words, customers may not tell you that they need an easy to use MP3 music player or what it should look like, but when Apple introduced an "easy to use" MP3 player, the iPod, customers swarmed all over it. If it had been no better than what was in the marketplace at the time, they would have rejected it. When you look to solve a customer problem, you need to validate that it's a real pain point with potential customers so that when you look to creative solutions, they actually need to solve the problem. The other thing you want to verify is your customer target segment. You can't really drive brainstorming sessions to come up with creative ideas to solve a problem if you don't clearly understand your customer target segment. Are they millennials, age 18 to 34, which will be the largest target segment in the USA by 2025 (81 million), or are they among the 71 million baby boomers, age 60 to 85, who today are still the largest customer segment in the USA? The key is knowing as much as you can about your customer before you start looking into discovering and solving their problems. Here are some simple tips that will help you learn more about your potential customers:

▲ **Observe them.** Hang out where they are and watch what they do; learn how they interact and purchase products and services you are looking to improve.

▲ **Walk in the customer's shoes.** Behave like your customer. Buy your product or service or a competitor's and see what the shopping experience is like. What did you learn from a customer perspective?

▲ **Talk to people closest to the customer.** Can you talk to the people who service or sell to the customer? What problems do they see? What problems do they hear about from customers?

▲ **Be a mole.** If you want to better understand or improve a product or service, then be your own "undercover boss" and learn what you don't know. Do a "ride along" in the customer environment or, if you can, shadow or be an employee for a day in the customer environment.

▲ **Talk to customers.** As simple as this advice seems, I cannot tell you how many corporate leaders and entrepreneurs I have met that just fall "out of touch" with their customers. Talk to your own or potential customers and listen for problems; then determine if you have a potential solution that meets their needs, not their wants.

The CreativityWorks Framework is a methodology for you to use in driving better creative ideas that could become innovative solutions. But you really can't create an innovative solution and move it into the marketplace unless you have a creative and persevering growth mindset, one that truly believes you can *be creative* and solve problems even when the rest of the world does not believe you.

CREATIVE / INNOVATIVE INSIGHT

This future entrepreneur was so poor that when his family emigrated from the Ukraine to the United States, he had to live on welfare and food stamps. However, the family thought of itself as lucky. Not everyone was able to escape this oppression and come to a place like the United States. A self-taught programmer, he worked for years in unglamorous roles at major tech companies in Silicon Valley.

He was a huge fan of Skype, because it allowed him to make long-distance calls for free. This gave him an idea to make something similar. He decided to develop a $1 iPhone app for sending free text messages anywhere in the world. The app's popularity at first wasn't clear. There were lots of free texting apps. But he kept at it, growing the business, improving the product, and staying true to the mission of providing free texting for just $1. He was told repeatedly that his app and company would never make it. After nearly five years of very hard work, Jan Koum sold his company, WhatsApp, to Facebook for $19 billion.

 Key Takeaway

You were not born to do anything. What you do is up to your growth mindset and perhaps your purpose. Have you embraced creativity in your life, and if so, have you found your purpose? If not, go find it.

CHAPTER THREE

MINDSET:
UNLEASH YOUR INNER CREATIVITY AND INNOVATION

As a young man, this future entrepreneur was fired from the *Kansas City Star* because his boss thought he lacked creativity. He went on to create a small entertainment company. Using his natural salesmanship abilities, he raised $15,000 in startup money; however, he made a deal with a New York distributor, and when the distributor went out of business, he was forced to shut down the company. He could barely pay his rent and even resorted to eating dog food.

Broke but not defeated, he spent his last few dollars on a train ticket to Hollywood. He started another entertainment company with a simple product idea. Unfortunately, his troubles were not over. As his new company gained traction, the distributors he relied on told him that one of his key projects would fail because the main character, a mouse, would "terrify women." Distributors rejected his next idea about three brothers with three houses because it needed more characters. They then rejected a project about a wooden puppet with a strange nose. But the entrepreneur believed he was creating a company that his customers would love because they could escape into the stories he was creating. And Walt Disney was right. His creativity, fueled by his "growth" mindset, combined with a lot of perseverance, created one of the best entertainment companies in the world.

THE SCIENCE OF A GROWTH MINDSET

Adopting a growth mindset is not just essential, it's critical. Those with a growth mindset understand that knowledge can be acquired and intelligence can be developed. With a growth mindset, people focus on improvement instead of worrying about how smart they are. They work hard to learn more and get smarter. Based on years of research by Dr. Carol Dweck and Lisa Blackwell PhD at Stanford University, we know that students who adopt this mindset show greater motivation in school and get better grades and higher test scores.

In one 2007 study, Blackwell and her colleagues followed hundreds of students making the transition to seventh grade. They found that students with a growth mindset were more motivated to learn and exert effort and outperformed those with a fixed mindset in math—a gap that continued to increase over a two-year period. Although all of the students had entered seventh grade with similar past achievement, their math grades pulled significantly apart during this challenging time because of their mindsets. In another study, Blackwell and her colleagues divided students into two groups for a workshop on the brain and study skills. Half of them, the control group, were taught about the stages of memory; the other half received training in the growth mindset (how the brain grows with learning to make you smarter) and how to apply this idea to their schoolwork. Three times as many students in the growth-mindset group showed an increase in effort and engagement compared with the control group. After the training, the control group continued to show declining grades (they were not keeping up with the new learning), but the growth-mindset group showed continued increases in their grades.

A "growth mindset" thrives on challenge and sees failure not as evidence of unintelligence but as a heartening springboard for growth and for stretching our existing abilities. A "fixed mindset," on the other hand, assumes that our character, intelligence, and creative ability are static givens that we can't change in any meaningful way. Out of these two mindsets, which we manifest from a very early age, comes our belief about whether or not we are creative. Here's the good news. No matter your current mindset, you can adopt and nurture a growth mindset.

Most people have one mindset or the other. Some of us have a combination. The good news is that we can all adopt a growth mindset simply by *putting ourselves in one*. It's easy to change. Just knowing about the two mindsets can make us think and act in new ways. Once we can spot the thoughts, words, and actions that go with the fixed and growth mindsets, we start catching ourselves in fixed mode and we can then learn to switch into growth mode. And once you know how to switch from a fixed to growth mindset, you can eventually stay there.

THE FIXED MINDSET

People with fixed mindsets believe they are limited to what they're born with in terms of intelligence and skill. They believe these things can't be developed much. It is possible to learn new things, but new learning doesn't change our basic level of intelligence.

It's possible to practice new skills, but our natural ability is really what's determinative. Some people are just "naturals" at certain things. They're good at things because "it's genetic." A fixed mindset tells us that people are however they are and not a lot can be done to change that. We should spend our energy doing what we're inherently good at. As a result, fixed-mindset people say things such as: "I am not athletic;" "I am bad at math;" "I can't spell;" "I have no discipline;" "I tried that already and it didn't work." Mostly they say, "I can't, I can't, I can't."

And what do they do? They do only what they're already good at. What they don't do is anything they haven't tried yet or that doesn't come easily. They avoid risk at all costs for fear of looking bad, making a mistake, or failing. They progress only for the sake of progressing instead of validating their self-worth. Dweck explains why: "[The fixed mindset] makes you concerned with how you'll be judged; the growth mindset makes you concerned with improving."

THE GROWTH MINDSET

People with growth mindsets, however, believe that intelligence and qualities we're born with are just the foundation for future development. They can be improved through learning and hard work. Some people can do certain things well with little or no training or practice, but others can learn to do those same things, just as well or better, with training and practice.

As a result, people with growth mindsets say things such as: "I have the rest of the week to get the project done." "I realized I had a choice: I could sit in my misery or I could do something about it." "All my life I've been playing up—I've challenged myself with players . . . older, bigger, more skillful, more experienced." "I don't walk on water. I just run faster than a lot of people."

And here's what they do: They try new things. They experiment, make mistakes, and correct them along the way. They reject what doesn't work after trying to see what might succeed. They tweak, iterate, and maintain an upward trajectory in effort and progress.

Here are some tips for transitioning from a fixed to growth mindset, all to drive your creativity potential:

- **Acknowledge and embrace imperfections.** Hiding from your weaknesses means you'll never overcome them. Pick a weakness and improve it by at least neutralizing it and, at best, turning it into a strength.

- **View challenges as opportunities.** Having a growth mindset means relishing opportunities for self-improvement. Learn more about how to fail well. Attack a small challenge until you succeed.

- **Try different learning tactics.** There's no one-size-fits-all model for learning. What works for one person may not work for you. Take an online course and learn a new language or skill.

- **Replace the word "failing" with the word "learning."** When you make a mistake or fall short of a goal, you haven't failed; you've learned. Instead of regretting a failure, study it for strategies to win in the future.

- **Stop seeking approval.** When you prioritize approval over learning, you sacrifice your own potential for growth. Do something well at work and don't tell anyone. Let the recognition come to you.

- **Value the process over the end result.** Intelligent people enjoy the learning process and don't mind when it continues beyond an expected time frame. I returned to school and got my MBA at age 52 so that I could teach at a university.

♦ **Emphasize growth over speed.** Learning fast isn't the same as learning well, and learning well sometimes requires allowing time for mistakes.

♦ **Reward actions, not traits.** Tell employees or colleagues when they're doing something smart, not just being smart.

♦ **Use criticism as a positive.** You don't have to use that hackneyed term "constructive criticism," but you do have to believe in the concept that being positive leads to learning.

♦ **Cultivate some grit.** People with that extra bit of determination and effort will be more likely to seek approval from themselves rather than others.

♦ **Take risks in front of others.** Stop trying to save face all the time and just let yourself admit that you're imperfect. It will make it easier to take risks in the future.

♦ **Own your attitude.** Once you develop a growth mindset, own it. Acknowledge yourself as someone who possesses a growth mentality and be proud to let it guide you throughout your career.

A GROWTH MINDSET FUELS CREATIVITY

Once you commit to a growth mindset, here are some things you can do immediately to fuel your creativity:

Draw something. Although we may have been reprimanded in school to "stop doodling and pay attention," it's time to bring back the doodle. Doodling, contrary to popular belief, does not demonstrate a lack of focus. In fact, doodling can help you stay present and engaged during an activity in which you might otherwise find your mind drifting. Sunni Brown, author of *The Doodle Revolution*, notes that some of the greatest thinkers—from Henry Ford to Steve Jobs— used doodling to jump-start creativity. Doodling can enhance recall and activate unique neurological pathways, leading to new insights and cognitive breakthroughs. For every exercise in my Creativity and Innovation class, students must draw the solution they choose to present from their brainstormed ideas. Always.

Sign up for a class in something new to you. Creativity flourishes when you push yourself outside of your comfort zone and learn something new. Many communities offer evening adult education classes. These classes are often very casual, with plenty of beginner offerings. Try painting, pottery, or woodworking. How about learning a new language, picking up a new instrument, or taking a cooking class? Anyone for learning how to code a mobile app? What can you adapt from that skill to your profession?

Create the right environment. Google goes to great lengths to provide its employees with fun perks such as beach volleyball courts and free beer, a setup almost resembling an adult playground. The goal is to create an environment that lets employees feel relaxed and comfortable with vocalizing creative, even wacky ideas. Businesses that value creativity need to do their best to foster a creative, safe space where unusual ideas are celebrated and where creativity is nurtured. What can you do tomorrow? Paint one wall in your office a bright cinnamon red. Don't have an office? Then put yourself into a coworking space that makes you feel creative.

Get up and get moving. If you're stuck developing an idea or even thinking of one, get unstuck by literally getting away from your desk. Go for a walk. Exercise. Bring your work somewhere else. Physical movement has been shown to have a positive effect on creative thinking. The philosopher and author Henry Thoreau claimed that his thoughts began to flow "the moment my legs began to move." Now scientists have discovered that taking part in regular exercise such as going for a walk or riding a bike really does improve creative thought. Professor Lorenza Colzato, a cognitive psychologist at Leiden University in the Netherlands, found in her 2013 study that people who exercised four times a week were able to think more creatively than those with a more sedentary lifestyle. One of my course sessions, an observation lab, is held outdoors, and the students love the walk and change in environment as they brainstorm possible solutions while moving across our San Diego campus. But you can always take a brainstorming group to other places, like a science or discovery museum or a great architectural space.

Start a sketchbook. Sketching is a great way to preserve memories and make constructive use of time that might otherwise be spent fiddling on a phone. Buy a small, lightweight sketchbook that can easily fit in your bag. Start sketching whenever you have even a few spare minutes—draw the salt and pepper shaker on your table while waiting for your coffee, or the crumpled pile of newspaper on the subway. Though you may be disappointed in your sketches at first, the more you draw, the better you'll get. Don't overanalyze your results—simply draw for the enjoyment of the process, not the end piece. Creativity seeps across activities, so sketching just a few minutes a day can result in a major boost of workplace creativity.

Keep toys on your desk. Many creative design companies encourage employees to keep toys on their desks—from Lego blocks and Lincoln Logs to Play-Doh and origami paper. Building something physically with your hands, as opposed to typing on a keyboard, can be just the creative jolt you need. If you were to visit employee offices at Google or Pixar, you would find some amazing workspaces with whimsical and personal decorations. One employee at Pixar converted his workspace into a real garden shed.

Try the thirty circles test. This great creative exercise comes from researcher Bob McKim and is featured in Tim Brown's TED talk on creativity and play. Take a piece of paper and draw thirty circles on the paper. Now, in one minute, adapt as many circles as you can into objects. For example, one circle could become a sun. Another could become a globe. How many can you do in a minute? (Take quantity over quality into consideration.) The result: Most people have a hard time getting to thirty, largely because we have a tendency as adults to self-edit. Children are great at simply exploring possibilities without being self-critical, whereas adults have a harder time. Sometimes, even the desire to be original can be a form of self-editing. Don't forget—good artists copy, great artists steal (and by "steal," T. S. Eliot meant transform in the theft and make one's own).

Skim through a magazine, online or offline. Visual aids can often help in the creative process, so skimming through a magazine relevant to what you're working on may help. For instance, if you're looking for design inspiration, page through a home improvement publication. If you want to make a delicious meal for houseguests, look through a cooking magazine. There are magazines for virtually everything you can think of, so you should be able to find something that piques your creativity rather easily. Or just roam through Pinterest randomly or with a purpose.

Anticipate the future. What's great about thinking about the future is that it's yet to be written. In your version, you're the author, which means there are endless possibilities. Tap into your creativity by thinking about life ten years from now. And think big, for goodness' sake. Your future will be what you make it. I was once asked in 2007 to write a manifesto on where technology would be taking us by 2015. It's really cool to see how you imagine the future from a present point of view. Working with clients? Write their ten-year industry manifesto. . . . What does it look like?

One of my biggest creative challenges in my career came while working on the Amazon account. Our agency had been tasked with coming up with the then startup's new marketing strategy, which included the identity (logo), a new website design, a complete integrated advertising campaign, a media strategy, and an affiliate strategy to get Amazon's square tile (affiliate commission link) on 50,000 websites. I pulled together the core team from our agency's Portland office and we spent several weeks working on defining the brand from a few different perspectives. One of the tasks we were struggling with was the possible "tagline" that would go with the new corporate identity to properly position the brand. Amazon in early 1996 did not have wide public awareness; most people had no clue what the company was or what it sold.

After three weeks of brainstorming sessions and rejecting more than 100 taglines and getting nowhere, I broke up the team and brought in three new people. They had no idea what Amazon did. One of the people on the team asked me a question: "How many books are in the average bookstore?" "About 50,000 titles," I said. He asked, "Where does Amazon get its books?" I replied that the books come from two key distributors, and the distributors themselves are massive and have quite a few books in inventory. "How many?" he asked. "More than a million titles," I replied. He said, "Wow, that would make Amazon Earth's biggest bookstore." That became our positioning line to launch the new campaign. *Amazon. com. Earth's Biggest Bookstore.*

At times to solve a problem, you might need to change your perspective or mix up the team. Sometimes it's the simplest questions that can lead to the biggest breakthroughs. Other times it is hard work. Either way, you need a growth mindset that believes you can solve the problem. Another thing you will need is an amazing environment, one driven by great leadership and culture (which we'll tackle in Chapter 4).

CREATIVE / INNOVATIVE INSIGHT

This startup team got one thing right when they got started: They loved working on solutions for software operating systems. They introduced security software for handheld PCs right as personal digital assistants (PDAs) started to come into the market. While their product was good, the handheld computer market did not take off. Then the team focused on creating an electronic wallet

(continued on next page)

(continued from previous page)

for PDAs. It turned out to be a great product, but again the product did not get much traction. Wrong timing, wrong marketplace. Then one of the team members heard that some people were using part of their software product on auction-based websites like eBay. But the team could not agree on what marketplace they should serve. One of the cofounders suggested they support these new online auction customers. The other cofounder thought this was a terrible idea because it was not the purpose for which they had designed the product. Another six months went by before the cofounders agreed to focus on the customers that loved their product. PayPal was born.

Key Takeaway

A creative growth mindset among a mission-driven team is an awesome thing. You will agree just as often as you will disagree. In the end, just remember to listen to your customers.

4

ENVIRONMENT MATTERS:
LEADERSHIP AND CULTURE

If a growth mindset is critical to driving creativity in the CreativityWorks Framework, then environment, which I define as
leadership plus culture, is probably the next most essential component. You can have the most creative people in the world but if
you don't give them the encouragement and space to thrive, the
company will go nowhere.

I saw this firsthand when our marketing agency helped Apple
launch Newton, a new type of personal digital assistant (PDA). I
am not going to question the timing of this product development
or whether the product actually had a customer segment waiting
for it. It was conceived and produced as an innovative forerunner
of handheld computers. The problem lay with what was happening at Apple at the time when Steve Jobs was not there. Even
with John Sculley as CEO, there was no real leadership and the
culture was dysfunctional at best. The senior vice presidents and
department managers from consumer to education to corporate

accounts were all fighting for their own share of the marketing dollars, and the product design leaders seemed lost turning out so many new products without a clear product strategy. There was no one person who approved product design and development the way Steve Jobs did when he was at Apple. The best way to describe it would be chaos.

Our agency was hired by Apple to handle the integrated marketing for the Newton product launch at about 6,000 retail locations in the USA. Key to our marketing effort was an interactive kiosk we designed and built (yes, 6,000 of them) for use at retail stores so that consumers could demo the Newton. The only problem was that Newton itself had so many bugs even as it approached the shipping date that it was crashing our demo software. We notified the project manager, who notified the director of the group, who notified the general manager of the division. Who promptly said, "Ship it."

I cannot describe to you the feeling among the Apple Newton project team and our agency team of about ten people. We knew the demo software would crash, rendering Newton to be basically a pretty piece of plastic sitting inside a beautifully designed retail kiosk. We knew the handwriting recognition software was not working properly. It seemed like madness. Who ships thousands of products knowing they are going to fail? A company that has no leadership and no real values or beliefs that is devoid of any meaningful culture. While the product was a failure, our agency executed the marketing campaign brilliantly, convincing 60,000 customers in the first ninety days to purchase a Newton that probably would not work. And that is what happened. The handwriting software and multiple bugs crashed the operating system, which essentially locked up the device continuously. The consumer outcry was deafening. Amazingly, our agency avoided any real negative fallout from this disastrous product launch. However, Apple was not so lucky. Apple continued to flounder, going through successive CEOs until Steve Jobs returned in 1997.

No matter what you think of Steve Jobs as a person, he led Apple from the brink of insolvency to again become one of the most innovative companies on the planet. In his first meeting with employees on his return, he indicated that Apple was not going to cut its way to profitability but innovate its way there. He immediately shifted focus to four products and introduced the "all in one" beautifully designed iMac to the world and sales took off. That's how much leadership and culture matter to a company.

Companies that are faced with rapid innovation in their industry have two choices. One, they can constantly innovate, even if it means eventually abandoning the original products or services (e.g., Starbucks now offers breakfast foods and juices and is introducing wine bars, etc.). Two, companies can choose to acquire a competitor or a startup. I guess there is a third choice, which is to do nothing or do all the wrong things. This is essentially what Kodak, Borders bookstores, and Blockbuster did. Quite frankly, what happened to the leadership at those three companies? How could the "captains" at those companies sit in their ships' towers and ignore the innovative "tips of the iceberg" they saw coming from competitors? All three ignored innovation in their industry and in effect steered their respective company ships right into the iceberg. Why? What were these executives thinking? They were running multibillion-dollar companies with thousands of employees. What happened to the innovative culture that made them successful in the first place?

THE INNOVATOR'S DILEMMA

If you keep doing what made you successful, you are a willing "slave" to your success. Until you are not successful. Clayton M.

Christensen was very curious about why companies failed. In his 1997 book, *The Innovator's Dilemma*, he argued that very often it isn't because company executives made bad decisions but because they made good decisions—the same kind of good decisions that had made those companies successful for decades. (The "innovator's dilemma" is that "doing the right thing is actually the wrong thing.") As Christensen saw it, the problem was the velocity of history, and it wasn't so much a problem as a missed opportunity, like a train that takes off without you, except that you didn't even know there was a train and you wandered onto the train tracks, which you thought was a cool hiking trail, and the train ran you over. For example, manufacturers of mainframe computers made good decisions about making and selling mainframe computers and devising important refinements to them in their R&D departments—"sustaining innovations," Christensen called them—but because they were busy pleasing their mainframe customers, one feature at a time, they missed what an entirely untapped customer wanted: personal computers. The PC market was created by what Christensen called "disruptive innovation": the selling of a cheaper, poorer-quality product that initially reaches less profitable customers but eventually takes over and devours an entire industry.

So, how do you avoid the "innovator's dilemma"? You need to be constantly paying attention to what's going on around you to the point of being obsessed with being put out of business by a competitor or even a new division you create. Andy Grove, the former CEO of Intel, had a great quote: "Only the paranoid survive." Once I heard this quote, I never forgot it. As a leader, don't be self-absorbed in your current innovation. Look over the horizon or behind you. Be paranoid in a good way. Self-disrupt or self-destruct or your competitors will do it for you.

The qualities and traits of good leadership, and the mistakes to avoid, are the focus of this chapter. You will learn more about company culture and how to create an amazing customer-driven culture in your own department or company. If you are not yet a leader, pay attention and start to adopt leadership qualities and traits now.

GROW YOUR LEADERSHIP QUALITIES AND TRAITS

I think everyone, at one time or another, wants to be a good leader. I don't care if it's in your local neighborhood or your corporate job or as a founder of a company; we want to be perceived by others as having the ability to lead. Unfortunately, good leaders are hard to come by. Why? Because, contrary to your own beliefs, you were not born with the knowledge or traits to be a leader. You learn how to be a leader through mentors, advisers, and experience. And you have to have a growth mindset, one that understands you will never stop learning and being curious. Let's look at the top qualities a leader might have.

Honesty: Whatever ethical plane you hold yourself to, when you are responsible for a team of people, it's important to raise the bar even higher. Your business and its employees are a reflection of yourself, and if you make honest and ethical behavior a key value, your team will follow suit.

Ability to Delegate: The art of executing your brand vision is essential to creating an organized and efficient business, but if you don't learn to trust your team with that vision, you might never progress to the next stage. It's important to remember that trusting your team with your ideas is a sign of strength, not weakness. Delegating tasks to the appropriate people is one of the most important skills you can develop as your business grows.

Ability to Communicate: Knowing what you want accomplished may seem clear in your head, but if you try to explain it to someone else and are met with a blank expression, you know there is a problem. If this has been your experience, then you may want to focus on honing your communication skills. Being able to clearly and succinctly describe what you want done is extremely important. If you can't relate your vision to your team, you won't all be working toward the same goal. Have an open-door policy and have employees feel they can come to you with anything. Create a feeling of trust with excellent two-way communications.

Ability to Laugh: If your product launches late, you lose that major client, or your funding dries up, guiding your team through the process without panicking is as challenging as it is important. Morale is linked to productivity, and it's your job as the team leader to instill positive energy. That's where your sense of humor will finally pay off. Encourage your team to laugh at the mistakes while learning from them instead of crying and wondering what to do next. If you find the humor in the struggles, your work environment will be happy and healthy. Employees will look forward to working in this environment, rather than dreading it.

High Degree of Confidence: There may be days when the future of your company is in jeopardy and things aren't going according to plan. This is true with any business, large or small, and the most important thing is not to panic. Part of your job as a leader is to put out fires and maintain the team morale. Keep up your confidence level and assure everyone that setbacks are natural and the important thing is to focus on the larger goal. By staying calm and confident, you will help keep the team feeling the same. Remember, your team will take cues from you, so if you exude a level of calm damage control, your team will pick up on that feeling. The key objective is to keep everyone working and moving forward.

Commitment: If you expect your team to work hard and produce quality content, you must lead by example. There is no greater motivation than seeing top leadership down in the trenches working alongside everyone else, showing that hard work is being done at every level. By proving your commitment to the brand and your role, you will not only earn the respect of your team, you will also instill that same hardworking energy among your staff. As a senior partner when our company was around $350 million in revenue, I came in on a weekend with other staff members to stuff envelopes for a major client. Walk the talk.

Positive Attitude: You want to keep your team motivated toward the continued success of the company and keep energy levels up. Whether that means providing snacks, coffee, relationship advice, or even just an occasional beer in the office, remember that everyone on your team is a person. Keep the office mood a fine balance between productivity and playfulness. If your team is feeling happy and upbeat, chances are they won't mind staying that extra hour to finish a project or really leaning in when you need them.

Open, Creative Mind: Some decisions will not always be so clear-cut. You may be forced at times to deviate from your set course and make on-the-fly decisions. This is where your creativity will prove to be vital. It is during these critical situations that your team will look to you for guidance and you may be forced to make a quick decision. As a leader, it's important to learn how to quickly come up with ideas that will potentially solve the problem. Don't immediately choose the first or easiest possibility; sometimes it's best to give these ideas some thought and even turn to your team for guidance. The key is to have an open creative mind.

Honed Instinct: Guiding your team through the process of day-to-day tasks can be honed to a T. But when something unexpected occurs, or you are thrown into a new scenario, your team will look to you for guidance. Drawing on past experience is a good reflex, as is reaching out to your mentors for support. Eventually, though, the tough decisions will be up to you to decide and you will need to depend on your experience and gut instinct for answers. Learning to trust yourself is as important as your team learning to trust you.

Ability to Inspire: Creating a business or launching a new product often involves quite a bit of trust. Especially in the beginning stages, inspiring your team to see the vision of the successes to come is vital. Make your team feel invested in the accomplishments of the company. Whether everyone owns a piece of equity or you operate on a bonus system, generating enthusiasm for the hard work you are all putting in is so important. Acknowledge the work that everyone has done and commend team members on each of their efforts.

Praise them in front of company leadership. Give them more responsibilities and encourage them to lead. It is your job to keep spirits up, and that begins with an appreciation for hard work. Celebrate the small successes. Always remind them of the big picture.

Being a leader today is different from what it was ten or twenty years ago. Today's workplace has a fast pace of change and many more demands. It also involves working with many teams usually across different time zones. It's a complex environment out there. Leading and managing have moved well beyond just commanding the troops to "get it done."

How many of these key leadership qualities and traits do you really have? Seriously, do your own audit and, no matter what, strengthen your leadership weaknesses. Discuss them with your mentor and work to remedy them. Now, let's take a look at the other important partner of environment—*culture*—and how great leadership can help create a great company culture.

BUZZ LIGHTYEAR AND COMPANY CULTURE

How does Pixar do it? One animated movie hit after another. I use the *Harvard Business Review* Pixar case in my Creativity and Innovation course not just to talk about a creative habitat (the topic of Chapter 5) but the leadership and "culture" that must exist to make it all work. You cannot mix art, technology, and design without purposely creating some healthy dissent among employees. And yet Pixar succeeds amazingly well. Based on my research, here are my top observations about the leadership and culture at Pixar, so many of which were also true for our own agency:

- Smart people are more important than good ideas.
- Create as many interactions between all types of people as possible.
- Everyone is a peer and there is no peer hierarchy.
- Everyone has the freedom to communicate with anyone.
- It must be safe for everyone to offer ideas.
- Stay close to innovations happening in the academic or industry community.
- Be introspective and try not to become irrelevant.

It sounds so simple, but if you look closely at the attributes of culture at Pixar, how many of these qualities even really exist at "normal" companies, Fortune 500 leaders, or chaotic startups? Having worked with a wide variety of companies in my career, I can only think of four or five companies that had great leadership and an amazing culture somewhat resembling what the leaders at Pixar have crafted. So how do you "engineer" a creative culture?

BREWING A CREATIVE COMPANY CULTURE

If innovation is important to the growth of your company, nothing will help you more than creating a company culture that is deliberately fluid and creative. No matter the size of your company, its industry, or your budget, certain environmental and behavioral changes are almost guaranteed to improve your team's creative output, attract the right talent, and ultimately move your company beyond what you can even imagine today.

Here are ten "observations," taken from my learnings with some great companies, that will help you create an amazing company culture:

1. **Inspire great work with an inspired workspace.** It all starts with the workspace. Remember the cubicle farms that emerged in the 1980s and 1990s? Quite a few still exist. But in today's design-centric, user-focused world, companies have to move quickly and innovate constantly, and that certainly won't happen from behind a beige cubicle wall and under dull overhead fluorescent light. Open spaces, living room setups, big windows, inviting kitchens, and convenient facilities like showers and bicycle parking are what's needed. Even if you aren't building an office from scratch, try adding bright colors or lots of whiteboards and markers. Providing your team with imaginative workspaces will help to nourish the outpouring of their creative juices.

2. **Be more flexible.** I'm sorry, does the world still work from nine to five? While stable work hours make for organizational order, creative energy cannot be simply willed into set hours. People have different rhythms that make them more or less productive during certain hours. If you want to encourage productivity and inspiration, allow flexible work hours for members of your team.

   Flexibility also attracts a creative talent pool of people with a variety of interests and commitments in life. I once recruited a highly talented web developer from San Francisco to Portland. He stayed at our home for two months in a guest cabana and usually rolled into work at the agency office around 11 a.m. Then he worked until midnight or later. My young son saw him so infrequently around our house, and never in the daytime, he once asked me if Nico was a vampire. No, just super creative.

3. **Allow unlimited vacation days.** I know this sounds crazy, but Netflix has been doing this for years and the company has amazing growth and high morale. The people on each team just hold each other accountable. And it works. Why? One of the surest ways to get inspired is to take a break from work. Inspiration is more likely to come when people are freed from the daily routine of familiar surroundings and motivated by new stimuli. Think about how many times you've had a brilliant idea during a flight or on a train ride or on a vacation. Offering your team unlimited vacation days—and taking them yourself—encourages not just "staycations" or a lazy beach break but also more experiential travel to faraway places that can open up a person to new ways of thinking.

4. **Build a diverse team.** Many business owners often complain that they have trouble finding good staff people. Perhaps what they're trying to find is a replica of themselves. They wrongly assume that having a professional twin would double their business overnight. Instead, build a diverse team whose strength lies in its members' range of work experience, education, and cultural backgrounds that play off of one another. In one technology company turnaround situation in 2001, I built a new marketing department where no one had any technology experience, but together the team members had what it took to successfully transition that company to a sale three years later for $110 million.

5. **Put your team first.** To have a truly creative company culture, your employees have to be your biggest priority. While you may think that your customers should always come first, take a cue from powerful CEOs like Virgin Group's Richard Branson, and Tony Hsieh of Zappos, along with Jim Sinegal

from Costco, who have proved that putting employees first makes customers and even shareholders happy. When asked by Wall Street analysts about high employee labor costs, Jim Sinegal would say that the order of priority, in order for Costco to be successful, was employees, then customers, and then investors. Based on Costco's current stock price, that seems to be working.

6. **Reward risk-taking.** Now that you've created time and a workspace to fuel creativity, further encourage it by rewarding risk-taking. Think of the companies that inspire you: How many of them achieved success by following tradition and sticking to the rules? Building your own company one day could be a huge risk. So why not surround yourself with people who can take risks to help further your vision? Companies like Google, Virgin, Apple, and others are dedicated to encouraging risk-taking behavior within a controlled environment. For example, Google allows employees to spend 20 percent of their time on nonwork-related projects. Truly disruptive ideas don't arise out of stability; allow a bit of chaos.

7. **Allow for disagreement.** Nothing fights complacency better than disagreement. You don't have to wage an internal office war or create psychological discord. No, disagreement between professionals is the foundation of debate, and debate is exactly what you need to make sure your company is constantly putting its best foot forward. Once, in our Portland agency office, I had a pretty strong disagreement with my other partner, the creative director, about the marketing strategy we were working on for Amazon. From my point of view he was just being stubborn for stubbornness' sake. After a full sixty minutes of arguing with him in his office and getting nowhere, I was so frustrated

about him ignoring the strategic points I was making that I felt I needed to make a defining statement. So, I tipped his desk over. Mad, then laughing, we had a pretty strategic conversation and came up with a strong marketing strategy for our client. The key is to not make it personal; fight for your point of view on the client's or the customer's behalf.

8. **Try mixing up your project team.** At a small company or in a department in a large company, people often have to help one another to complete big projects. Someone from the design team might end up working with someone from the technology group. Creating a situation where people with entirely different skill sets and perspectives must work together can stimulate the best type of creativity and bring unexpected breakthroughs in thinking.

9. **Don't hurt anyone but be direct.** Discourage the need for diplomacy. Let people voice what they feel. Encourage your team members to talk openly rather than worrying about being "nice" or whether they hurt the feelings of others. Create a culture where employees ask tough questions of one another without being defensive. This ensures that people don't fall into complacency and are constantly thinking and talking about only the most relevant issues and problems and asking the smartest questions. And that means being focused on solutions your customers need.

10. **Provide some freedom and inspire responsibility.** At a small company with a big vision or at a big company with small departments, even the most junior employees bear a lot of responsibility. Hold people accountable to big expectations but be ready to give them the autonomy to make their own

decisions (with minimal guidance). This creates an atmosphere of resourcefulness and scrappiness that strongly supports creativity. In helping to create our company, all I ever wanted was to be able to lead the creative strategy and solutions for our clients and customers, not be micromanaged by someone in Cleveland (no disrespect to people from Cleveland). Of course, I will then be responsible for my decision making. No problem.

Great leadership and culture go hand in hand. You usually can't have one without the other. And when they feed off each other, you have created a place where creativity can flourish and problem solving is the everyday norm. And that environment will potentially ignite innovation.

LEADERSHIP AND CULTURE LEAD TO INNOVATION

As a current or potential leader you need to have employees feel motivated that they will succeed and achieve. More important, you need to give them the creative freedom to do what they need to do; it gives them a counterbalance to those redundant tasks that have to be completed well in a normal day. As a leader, you want to engage employees and bring a positive atmosphere to the company because it makes the job a lot easier and sparks creative problem solving, which can spark innovation. Without your creative leadership, you won't have a creative atmosphere. Your role is to enthusiastically engage employees in the company's mission. When employees feel engaged it betters the company culture; people will want to do more for the company and make sure that they are pleasing their bosses and their peers. They feel as if they're a part of a strong team on an important mission.

However, when employees aren't engaged and their leaders don't do anything to correct matters, work becomes a grueling slog and the office more a prison than a fun place to learn and create new ideas that solve customer needs. One Mayo Clinic study found that for each one-point increase in composite leadership score, there was a commensurate 3.3 percent decrease in likelihood of burnout and a 9 percent increase in the likelihood of job satisfaction. Think about how that translates into bottom-line dollars—less attrition and turnover, higher patient/client satisfaction scores, and a reduced instance of errors. Leadership decides how the workplace will take shape; it's what separates the weak companies from the great ones. That's why when you hear of amazing company leaders, you imagine people with a clear, transparent, and fun company that other people want to go work at. Leaders make companies thrive. If you're a leader or want to be one, make sure that you're doing your best to motivate and inspire others, as you will drive your company's creative culture.

Leadership and culture have a huge impact on employees' "mindset," but there is another attribute of the CreativityWorks Framework that only makes it better—habitat. That's a subject I will cover in Chapter 5.

CREATIVE / INNOVATIVE INSIGHT

This company had a meteoric rise from its founding, creating a brand so powerful that some people felt they could not live without their products. As the company grew, the founder brought in senior managers and groomed his replacements. All seemed well. Then several things happened simultaneously soon after the founder left the day-to-day operations. Investors in the public company wanted more, and when sales revenue slowed, the stock price got hammered down. Then the 2008 recession hit. The founder looked around and did not even see his original company. He decided to step back into the company as the CEO. He wrote a frank and honest letter to all employees and visited hundreds of retail locations. He finally admitted the company had lost what it once had and had stopped listening to customers and innovating. He bravely put into action a strategic plan to get back the company's "mojo" and to once again be a market leader. He restored original traditions, looked at customer trends, and acquired tea, juice, and bakery companies, extending the company's original product line and better serving customers' needs. Howard Schultz was back as the company's leader. Starbucks was back.

Key Takeaway

As a company, it does not matter how big you become. Your size does not insulate you from mediocrity or the competition. Never stop meeting and exceeding your customers' needs and innovating your brand forward. If you don't, the competition happily will.

CHAPTER FIVE

HABITAT:
YOUR SURROUNDINGS ARE KEY

I don't care what any analyst says about how much money can be saved by packing people into a sixty-square-foot workspace. You can never underestimate the power of an environment that potentially inspires people to do more. It doesn't matter what business you are in, either.

Our marketing agency has its roots in Silicon Valley, and we wanted to be one of the best creative marketing agencies in the world. As we grew and opened more offices, we paid careful attention to how our offices and workspaces looked. What was the literal and "unconscious" message we were sending to potential clients and, more important, to our employees? The same. The best creative stuff in the world happens here. When you have people *aspire* to do the best creative work, they are *inspired* to do the best creative work.

As Ed Catmull, president of Pixar, wrote in his book, *Creativity Inc.*, with respect to Steve Jobs, "What's our most important function? It's the interaction of our employees. That's why Steve put everyone in one building. He wanted to create a place for people to always be talking to each other."

You may have a limited budget, but you do not have a limited imagination. There are three core things in a physical space that don't have to cost a lot to make it a more creative space:

1. **The Ceiling:** Open it up and go as high as you can. No ceiling tiles.
2. **The Floor:** Use wood or polished cement for flooring. No regular carpet.
3. **The Walls:** Splash some color on the walls. Put up a six-foot clock and scrabble mosaic.

With a creative space, you create a sense of opportunity or destiny for employees. They "feel" they are supposed to be creative and innovative. So they push the boundaries and the creative envelopes. Why? Because they feel they are supposed to.

CREATIVE HABITAT NEEDS LEADERSHIP AND CULTURE

Scott Berkun, author of *The Myths of Innovation*, wrote in a blog post that a well-designed workplace may be beneficial, but it's not an essential factor. The long history of innovation, in the centuries before electricity and elevators, shows how much creative work can be done without regard to workspace design. A huge percentage of innovations took place in environments that fail most of the standards for "creative workplaces" or "dynamic work environments." As examples, Berkun points to any company (Google, Apple, HP, Amazon, Disney) and any band that started in a garage (Nirvana, The Kinks, Creedence Clearwater Revival).

The Wright brothers worked in a bike shop, and the Internet and the Web emerged from ordinary academic research labs, and so on. Put simply, Berkun writes, a good team will be productive in a cave. A bad team will be miserable in the most creative space in the world.

A good leader of any company should want to provide the best possible creative environment for employees. But the primary reason great work happens might have little to do with the creative characteristics of workplace design. Some people achieve great work in very ordinary and unremarkable settings. The reason might have more to do with a sense of mission coupled with strong leadership and culture.

GREAT WORKSPACES CAUSE COLLISIONS

A key element of a "creative" workspace is its ability to cause "collisions" between employees, hopefully from multiple departments of the company. At a startup, you probably don't have this problem because your space is likely small enough so that everybody runs into everyone all day long. But if you manage one department among many or if you lead a large organization, you should be focused on creating more interactions between employees from multiple departments. Research shows that the higher the number of interactions, the higher the potential impact on the company's bottom line. If you don't encourage or facilitate these interactions, people may not move from their "areas," making everyone exiles together.

The 2010 Ernst & Young study "Connecting Innovation to Profit," as cited by *Psychology Today*, concluded that "the ability to manage, organize, cultivate, and nurture creative thinking is directly linked to growth and achievement." The American

Psychological Association has also connected creativity to company growth. In one study, a group of employees in Orange County, California, participated in creativity training. According to the study, "Eight months later, the employees had increased their rate of new idea generation by 55 percent, resulting in more than $600,000 in new revenue and $3.5 million in savings from innovative cost reductions." But don't just focus on creativity; create more employee collisions.

In his seminal 1977 book, *Managing the Flow of Technology*, Thomas J. Allen was the first to measure the strong negative correlation between physical distance and frequency of communication. The "Allen curve" estimates that we are four times as likely to communicate regularly with someone sitting six feet away from us as with someone sixty feet away, and that we almost never communicate with colleagues on separate floors or in separate buildings. So, how do you get people from various departments or with different skill sets colliding?

DESIGNING THE WORKSPACE FOR MAXIMUM INTERACTIONS

Steve Jobs famously redesigned the offices at Pixar, which originally housed computer scientists in one building, animators in a second building, and executives and editors in a third. Jobs recognized that separating these groups, each with its own culture and approach to problem solving, discouraged them from sharing ideas. The solution was one building with a central atrium, designed to encourage employee collaboration. Perhaps the animators could introduce a fresh perspective when the computer scientists became stuck; maybe the executives would learn more about the nuts and bolts of the business if they occasionally met an animator in the office kitchen or a computer scientist at the watercooler. As Walter

Isaacson writes in his biography of Jobs, the Pixar building was designed to promote encounters and unplanned collaborations. "If a building doesn't encourage that, you'll lose a lot of innovation and magic that's sparked by serendipity," Jobs said. "So we designed the building to make people get out of their offices and mingle in the central atrium with people they might not otherwise see." The front doors and main stairs and corridors all lead to a central atrium, where a café and employee mailboxes are located as well.

Jobs ultimately succeeded in creating a single cavernous "office" that housed the entire Pixar team, and John Lasseter, Pixar's chief creative officer, declared that he'd "never seen a building that promoted collaboration and creativity as well as this one." Let's take a closer look at the core elements of the Pixar workspace:

Promotes Unplanned Collisions: One important element of the Pixar campus is its large atrium space. Steve Jobs believed that unplanned employee interactions and collaborations were vitally important to the company culture; this atrium space was to act as a melting pot of meeting spaces. He even wanted the atrium to house the only campus restrooms to force such collaboration.

Mixes Different Departments: As a part of the Pixar campus, Jobs envisioned the atrium bringing the different departments together. Animators could talk to storyboarders. Sound technicians could talk to computer scientists. And everyone would be pushing each other on toward their goal—but doing so in an environment where employees see fresh faces and have interactions that spark new creative ideas.

Encourages Employee-Designed Workspaces: Pixar's employees decorate their offices to their own satisfaction. In terms of decoration and style, employee office spaces are a sight to be seen. Some are small house huts; others are shared spaces. John Lasseter's office is filled to the brim with toys—clearly not your average executive office. If you were to walk around downstairs in the animation area, you'd see that it is not your normal office space, either. People are allowed to create whatever "front" to their office they want. One employee might build a front that's like a Western town. Someone else might do something that looks like Hawaii. Lasseter believes that if you have a loose, free kind of atmosphere, it helps creativity. I would agree.

Offers Reminders of Successes: Creating a work environment that people enjoy working in can be one of the most challenging aspects of modern office design. And surely one of the most memorable features at Pixar is the many characters, big and small, that find their way around the campus. Outside you'll find a huge version of Luxo Jr., while within the atrium you'll see the cast of *The Incredibles* and *Monsters Inc.* Why? Sure, it adds some brand value to a campus that otherwise might seem plain, but for a company like Pixar, whose employees work for many years bringing their films to life, I think it represents a connection to and love of their work. There can be no greater feeling than walking around the workplace and being reminded of the great work you helped to produce—as well as seeing the smiles of the many visitors as they recollect the ways each movie touched their lives.

You may not work at a "Pixar-like" company, but look at what the collective leadership at Pixar has created. The company's leaders have actually designed a workspace that moves projects along more creatively and probably faster than if all these people worked in separate buildings. How many of us have worked in companies where people from one department never even met people from another department? Do we know or sense that a loss of productivity or opportunity has to be associated with that kind of environment? Research and experimentation is starting to prove how valuable increased interactions are between employees.

One pharmaceutical company wanted to determine if an increase of collaborations between sales and various departments would increase sales. So the question executives asked was, "How can we change our space to get the sales staff running into colleagues from other departments?" In this case, the answer was coffee. At the time, the company had roughly one coffee machine for every six employees, and the same people used the same machines every day. The sales force commiserated with itself. Marketing people talked to marketing people. Researchers talked to researchers. And so on. The company invested several hundred thousand dollars to rip out the coffee stations and build fewer, bigger ones—just one for every 120 employees housed in more central locations. It also created a large cafeteria for all employees in place of a much smaller one that few employees had used. In the fiscal quarter after the coffee-and-cafeteria switch, sales rose by 20 percent, or $200 million.

KEY ELEMENTS OF A CREATIVE HABITAT

No matter what kind of company you are in or what kind of new company you plan to create, it's important to remember how critical habitat or workspace is to your company mission. You don't need to be a space designer to understand the benefits of your employees having more interactions and possible collaborations, whether to solve problems or to generate new products or services. Here are the key elements that make for a collaborative creative habitat:

- An open floor plan and other design features (e.g., high-traffic staircases, atriums that connect departments) that encourage accidental interactions
- More common areas than are strictly necessary; multiple cafeterias, other places to read and work that encourage workers to leave confined offices
- Emphasis on areas that hold two or more people, rather than single-occupancy offices
- Purpose-free generic "thinking" areas in open-plan spaces, which encourage workers to do their thinking in the presence of other people, rather than alone

It's kind of amazing how the first three elements of the CreativityWorks Framework—mindset, environment (leadership and culture), and habitat—are so closely intertwined. We tend not to really understand how we, individually, can impact creativity and innovation, but, like most things, we can break it down into understandable pieces of knowledge. And with that knowledge comes the power of understanding that we truly can make a difference in how a company becomes and remains innovative on purpose. We can purposely engage creative, diverse people on a common mission in a great environment.

Before we go into brainstorming, the fourth element of the framework, in Chapter 6 we'll review the importance of dynamic teams.

CREATIVE / INNOVATIVE INSIGHT

In the late 1940s, two psychologists and one sociologist began to wonder how friendships form. Why do some work "strangers" build lasting friendships while others struggle to get past basic platitudes? Some experts, including Sigmund Freud, explained that friendship formation could be traced to infancy, where children acquired the values, beliefs, and attitudes that would bind or separate them later in life. But these three researchers pursued a different theory. The researchers believed that physical space was the key to friendship formation; that "friendships are likely to develop on the basis of brief and passive contacts made going to and from home or walking about the neighborhood." In their view, it wasn't so much that people with similar attitudes became friends, but rather that people who passed each other during the day tended to become friends and later adopted similar attitudes. They conducted a study using a unique working lab environment at Massachusetts Institute of Technology (MIT), and the results were fascinating because they had very little to do with values, beliefs, and attitudes. Rather, friendships had everything to do with people's close proximity to each other and their level of interactions. People within sixty feet of each other had a greater likelihood of becoming friends. This idea that proximity and interactions created friendships went on to affect the founders of Pixar, Google, and Facebook as they all built their offices and campuses to not only evoke creativity but to create as many interactions as possible during the day between their employees.

Key Takeaway

The company workspace should not be a drab place for people to work until they go home. It should be a creative place designed for people to create, solve problems, and work together in a shared "neighborhood" while on an innovative mission. At a minimum, figure out how to increase the frequency of employee "collisions."

CHAPTER SIX

TEAMS ARE CRITICAL:
ASPIRATION AND MISSION

I slowly put the phone back into its cradle. It was a beautiful spring day and the sun was shining. During the phone call, which lasted about ten minutes, I had sweated through my dress shirt. I had removed my tie about two minutes into the call. On the other end of the call was my client, the VP of marketing at a large retail brand who, after screaming at me for what seemed like hours, calmly informed me that their company was suing our marketing agency for more than $10 million, and it could conceivably rise to $100 million. The problem was a mistake we made on their marketing campaign. So I leaned back, stunned into submission, and pondered exactly how I was going to tender my resignation. I thought, "Why was this happening to me? How did this happen?" Frankly, it was all related to me not knowing how to select, train, and lead a team. Let me explain.

I was hired into the marketing agency about three years earlier in my first professional job. It was a great opportunity. The agency was growing rapidly, I had come out of college late and so I put myself on a fast track. After just three years, I was an account director and a rising star. I worked crazy hours, seventy-five to ninety hours per week; the first year at the agency I worked six to seven days a week, spending weekends learning how to program so that I could do my own custom report queries on several databases that housed our client's customer data. My personal belief was that all my success would come from my abilities to make it happen. I did not really believe other people were as smart or as competent as me. I truly believed that to get things done right, you had to do them yourself.

So when we landed a large retail brand, I was thinking, "Man, if I get this account right, I am going to get promoted to be a vice president." And when I was asked to take on this new account and hire a team to run it, I was ecstatic. Then, having never really managed a team before, I proceeded to make every mistake you could regarding hiring, training, and leading one.

First, I hired people like me, but not quite as smart as me, lest I feel threatened. Second, all seven team members reported directly to me, and I micromanaged the hell out of them. Third, I did not let anyone on the team make a decision without my input.

So, in hindsight, it was pretty predictable that my own inability to understand the potential and nature of a great team would lead to a catastrophic mistake. The team, through a series of seemingly small decisions, had created the situation for the error that occurred. But it was my fault. I never trusted the team. They were trying to do the right thing and they made a mistake. But I took the hit. The CEO of the marketing agency taught me a very valuable lesson. He did not fire me. He invited me to his house for what I thought was going to be the grand execution, but instead he spent five hours with me dissecting how the problem happened and, in the process, exposing a key flaw in my management style. The

CEO made me understand that my future career success would ultimately come from the fact that everything in business is done by teams. And that great teams do the best work. That night, I vowed to be a leader of great teams.

Amazingly, I actually recovered from this marketing mistake with the retail brand. We found a way to legally remedy the error and we did not get sued. We did lose the account, but we professionally managed it over the next ninety days to successfully transition it to another agency. Nothing brings your ego down to earth like cleaning up your own mess. I continued on at the agency for another four years, built great teams, and achieved even greater success. All without working crazy hours anymore. I'd learned that working "smart" was better than working "hard."

INDIVIDUALS CAN START COMPANIES, BUT TEAMS BUILD THEM

If you are wondering why I have a chapter on teams in a book on creativity and innovation, it's because teams are critical to both. But we don't really teach people the skill sets related to recruiting, training, and leading a great team. Even in my college-level Creativity and Innovation course, students complain about their project teams all the time. "She does not show up for meetings;" "He does not do so-and-so;" "They don't like me." I tell the students the same thing I tell businesspeople I mentor: Get over it. Make your "team work." It's life. Teams are never perfect but learning how to manage and lead teams is priceless.

Let's look at the importance and benefits of teams:

▲ **No employee can work alone for long.** You have to work with colleagues to accomplish a task efficiently, with each person bringing his or her particular best to bear on the task. Think Apollo 13. It took the astronauts and NASA's Mission Control working together to get the spacecraft back to Earth. One person didn't just turn the ship around.

▲ **Problems are more easily solved.** A single brain can't always come up with solutions or make decisions. In a team, every team member can contribute varying alternatives that another person might not have struck upon. You can then bring your different points of view to a discussion of the alternatives and come up with the best possible solution.

▲ **Tasks are accomplished more quickly.** An individual will definitely take more time to perform if that person is single-handedly responsible for everything. When employees work together, they start helping each other and responsibilities are shared, and thus it reduces the workload and work pressure. Team members can be assigned one or the other responsibility according to their specialization and level of interest, and thus the output is much more efficient and faster. There's a reason Henry Ford's assembly line was so successful.

▲ **Work never suffers or takes a backseat.** On critical projects, you need to manage your "bus factor." That is, how many people can get "hit by a bus" before the project comes to a screeching halt. In a team, the other team members can perform and manage the work in the absence of any member and therefore work is not affected much. The team keeps the project moving forward.

It's okay for there to be healthy competition among team members. Competition is always good for employees as well as the organization because people feel motivated to perform better than their other team members (or to be perceived as being valuable to the team) and in this way contribute even more to the team. And collectively the team outperforms. On the NHL ice hockey team the Chicago Blackhawks, Jonathan Toews celebrates as much when he scores as when Patrick Kane, his teammate, does.

Teamwork is also important to improve the camaraderie among employees. Individuals who work in close coordination with each other come to know each other better. The level of bonding increases as a result of teamwork. Research shows when team members care about one another, they perform better.

Team members can also gain knowledge more rapidly when they work together than when they work alone. Every individual is different and has some unique qualities and skill sets and knowledge. Each individual can benefit by learning something new from other team members, which would actually help them in the long run. Would there have been a Google if Larry Page had not met Sergey Brin, and how much did they learn from each other working together out of a garage in Menlo Park, California?

Working on a team increases accountability. Peer pressure is a powerful force. Particularly if you're working with people you respect and don't want to let down. The motivation to help your team succeed can help you overcome those down days when you're not at your best.

The lows of a project are more demoralizing when working alone. Sand traps that you struggle to get out of, monotonous work that you need to grind through, and problems that seem to defy all understanding become less draining and more bearable when there's someone else to share the pain with. And celebrating an achievement with teammates is a great way to boost morale. If you work alone, who are you going to high-five when you get something right?

All of this doesn't mean that working on or leading a team is easy. We've all probably had our share of project experiences where slackers don't pull their own weight and take the fun out of teamwork. But given the productive results of great teams, you should figure out and practice how to build effective teams.

BUILD YOUR OWN GREAT TEAM

Let's say you are challenged to building your own great team, whether it's for a department or a startup company. What does your team look like and what type of people comprise the team? Here's a sample roster:

▲ **The Genius:** Expertise is one skill a founding team can't do without. Often a diva, the genius will challenge the rest of the team and ask for things that the others aren't sure how to get done. This person is filled with passion and is often considered to be the most high-risk member of the team. Geniuses ask for a lot, and they never settle.

▲ **The Overperformer:** The overperformer is the person who gets down to business and accomplishes tasks. From ordering office supplies to keeping the office network running, this person has a combination of eccentricity, nerdiness, and charisma. The genius and the overperformer are often the same type of person. Add this person as early to your team as possible as this personality is nearly impossible to add later. Too disruptive.

▲ **The Team Leader:** Running a team or company with more than one founder is a democratic process, but hard decisions that affect everyone need to be made. Consensus usually requires compromise. Every project team or startup needs a clear leader. Leaders aren't necessarily paid more or have more equity, and they're not necessarily the CEO. The leader is just someone whom the others look up to and are willing to follow if there is conflict and when tough decisions need to be made.

▲ **The Industry Expert:** While departments or startups are often formed around new ideas, it helps to have someone who knows how things are done in the company's industry. It takes a long immersion in the marketplace to call yourself an insider, to understand the subtleties of the competitive landscape, to recognize people as true assets, and to cut through the "noise" in the industry and clearly see the opportunity. The industry expert has been there, seen it, and knows what to do.

▲ **The Sales Beast:** Startups, new departments, or growing companies with brilliant ideas often forget that someone needs to sell something. Having a strong salesperson on the team helps minimize the risk. The combination of technical insight, leadership, and sales experience is a hard-to-beat advantage in a competitive marketplace. This person could seemingly sell anything to anybody at any time. Just make sure this person has a high degree of integrity to go with his or her "beast" sales mode.

▲ **The Financial Nerd:** Every project team, startup, or rapidly growing company needs to budget, manage resources carefully, and predict cash flow, which means it needs financial talent. While this might be the easiest personality to add, the financial expert could also be one of the most important people on the team, especially if managing finances is critical to the team's success.

TEAM MISSION, ASPIRATIONS, AND RISK ARE CRITICAL

Since learning from the mistakes I made with my first team, I've worked with amazing teams for the rest of my career. One tool that can help you build great teams is the three team domains framework from *The New Business Road Test*, 4th edition, by John Mullins, a professor at the London School of Business and a former entrepreneur. It will enable you to build teams for your department, division, or startup intentionally as opposed to letting them randomly come together.

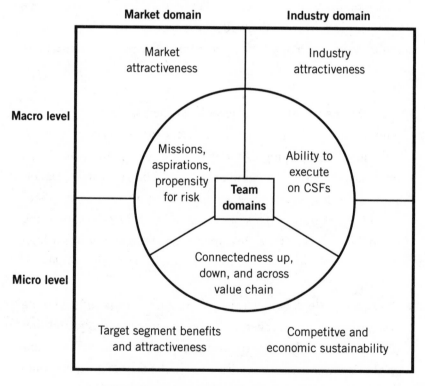

[MULLINS'S THREE TEAM DOMAINS FRAMEWORK]

Team Domain One: Mission, Aspirations, Propensity for Risk

In this domain, located in the center of Mullins's model, you are going to analyze commitment—yours and that of your team—to this department, startup, or idea. If it is a startup, think about why you want to start this business. Are you passionate about this idea and, if so, why? What do you want to do with this business? Are you ambitious for it, or do you want it to be a "lifestyle business"? What are your personal goals and values, and how does this venture align with them? And are you prepared to take the risk and put in the hard work needed to build this business? Explore the motivations of your team, too. What are they hoping to achieve and why? Do their motivations align with yours? And are they prepared to work really hard to make the business a success? Money and/or reputations could be at stake if the venture fails, so think about attitudes toward risk within the team.

Team Domain Two: Ability to Execute on Critical Success Factors

You now need to identify the critical success factors (CSFs) for the business or project and think realistically about whether your team can deliver on them. Start by answering these questions:

+ Which decisions or activities will harm the business significantly if you get them wrong, even when everything else is going right?
+ Which decisions or activities will deliver disproportionately high benefits or enhance performance, even if other things are going poorly?
+ Given the knowledge and skills of the team that you've put together, how certain are you that you and your team

can deliver successfully on these CSFs? If you see a gap in skills or abilities, who can you bring on board to fill this gap?

Team Domain Three: Connectedness Up, Down, Across the Value Chain

This last domain is all about your network and industry connections and how important they are to the success of your business. First, look at your suppliers and potential investors. Who do you know who can supply you with the resources you need to pursue this venture? How good are your relationships with these people? Next, look at your potential customers and distributors. In what ways can you capitalize on your connections here? Last, look across the value chain, including product development, manufacturing, and distribution. Who do you or your network know across the value chain? Do you know any of your competitors personally? If so, how could this relationship help or hinder your venture? And could these people be partners if you thought about them differently?

All too often, when I meet with founding teams or managers of departments in existing companies, it does seem rather random how these teams were created. They seem to be based rather loosely on friendships as opposed to skill sets. While working with your friends can be good or bad, depending on what happens and on the team domain variables, a great team would seem to be one that is put together strategically. Remember, assembling a great team will lead to a higher level of creativity regarding problem solving and potentially innovation.

Let me share another perspective on team "mission" with you, one that I use in my Creativity and Innovation course.

WHAT'S YOUR MISSION?

One thing I have learned in working with creativity and innovation tools/frameworks is that the quality of the team and the pace of the mission are directly correlated to the team's potential for success. In Silicon Valley, most top venture capitalists (VCs) say, "Give me a great team with a decent or even mediocre idea and they will figure it out. A weak team with a great idea is a recipe for disaster." In my Creativity and Innovation course, student teams get more done in a demanding forty-five-minute structured brainstorming exercise than if I gave them hours or days to solve the problem. In other words, a team with no deadline or sense of mission tends to become lazy and meandering in solving a problem. A talented and creative team with a limited time frame and looming deadline gets things done with a sense of urgency.

Why are some teams creative and actually push for innovative breakthroughs and why do others go nowhere? Urgency. Let's look at four types of teams and their potential for creativity based on the "urgency" of their mission and the creative makeup of the team:

[CREATIVITY AND MISSION GRID]

	Low Pressure	High Pressure
High Creativity	Journey	Get There Now
Low Creativity	Cruise Control	Daily Grind

▲ **The Cruise Control Mission:** Absolutely the worst scenario for potential innovation. There is a low amount of pressure to get anything done, so you end up with a team with low creativity aspirations.

▲ **The Daily Grind Mission:** This type of team is marginally better than the previous one, with the difference being that the pressure is high for the team to perform perhaps by a certain deadline. The problem is that the team is not very creative, talent-wise, so they feel the pressure but don't know how to solve the problem. So team members tend to stand still and grind in place.

▲ **The Journey Mission:** This team actually has a high amount of creativity, which is awesome, but there's low pressure to perform, no real deadline, and no end in sight for the project, so team members tend to meander and wander around. The result is several creative starts and stops with no real destination.

▲ **The "Get There Now" Mission:** This team, with a high amount of creativity and a high pressure deadline, has the highest potential to be both creative and innovative. They may have limited time and resources but they are highly creative, can pivot if necessary, and when facing an imposing deadline, they figure out how to get it done. This is the best possible team; they are highly creative under pressure and when facing a deadline.

Once I learned how to build, nurture, and lead great teams, what we accomplished was amazing. The crazy thing was, the more I praised individual team members to their face or to my senior partners, the more credit I received. My senior partners would say, "Yeah, but you hired and led that team. We know they are amazing. But it's your confidence and trust in the team that makes you a great leader. And you get everything done well and on time. Clients love you.

Keep it up." It took me some time early in my career to realize that the potential of my career success would be based on other people accomplishing tasks and projects for which I was accountable. Once I understood this, my career opportunities exploded.

For instance, the team we built for the Amazon account was incredible. The team had to define a new marketplace, conduct the research, understand this new thing called the Internet, create the campaign, and unleash the marketing in less than ninety days, all while working directly with Jeff Bezos (who had no marketing employees at the time) and with his venture capitalists constantly questioning our marketing strategy. What a rush. What a great team. Oh, and I think Amazon did okay.

Invariably, every team faces challenges and problems. And in order to solve those problems or overcome a challenge, they need to collectively understand the real problem and then generate ideas to solve the problem. Almost every team will turn to brainstorming at some point. And so many brainstorming sessions are like "idea contests" with no real structure or framework. In Chapter 7, I will share with you my point of view on brainstorming—that is, why you should only do brainstorming with a "tool" and a defined framework and not as some random group think. Then, in subsequent chapters, I will share some amazing brainstorming tools and a powerful framework.

CREATIVE / INNOVATIVE INSIGHT

The founder of this company had a passion and perhaps an idea, but needed what he did not know he needed: a team. The founder grew up in the New York area; he led

(continued on next page)

(continued from previous page)

a rather normal life, went to college, and then became a DJ. He loved music and hung around with people who loved music and art. Once, he wrote a letter to a very popular DJ duo in Europe asking them how much would they charge to come to New York and play their music. The DJ duo replied that they needed "$15,000 and two first-class plane tickets." The founder had no money but instinctively knew people in New York would pay to see the DJ duo. But he did not have the resources and so no DJ duo. Still, the experience sparked an idea: What if there was a collective voice, rather than an individual one, that could come together and pool their financial resources? Over the next few years, he noodled and refined the idea but it never went anywhere. Then he met a freelance musician and told him of his idea. For the next two years, both of them pursued "the idea," drawing and sketching out how it would work. Finally, they met a designer and showed him their drawings. The designer went to work and built a website. They launched the website to help filmmakers and artists get their projects funded from a collective voice. Kickstarter was born.

Key Takeaway

Ideas are great, and while a founder can come up with an idea to start a company, you need a team to build a company. And if the "team" has the mutual passion to be on a mission, then you might create something great.

CHAPTER 7

BRAINSTORMING RULES AND PRACTICES

I have been in hundreds, if not thousands, of brainstorming meetings. Most were not constructive. I'm sure my experience is not unique, so I imagine you can understand why: The sessions did not start with an agreed-on problem by the group or an identified structure; instead, the people running the sessions simply allowed the attendees to hear themselves share a bunch of random ideas. Brainstorming, however, can be a powerful tool for creativity if pursued correctly. So let's review how brainstorming began and why it's essential, the key components of effective brainstorming, and the best practices for a session. Then in the subsequent chapters I will introduce you to some amazing brainstorming tools.

AN ADMAN INVENTS BRAINSTORMING

In the late 1940s, Alex Osborn, a partner in the advertising agency BBDO, decided to write a book in which he shared his creative secrets. At the time, BBDO was widely regarded as the most innovative firm on Madison Avenue. Born in 1888, Osborn had spent much of his career in Buffalo, where he started out working in newspapers. His life at BBDO began when he teamed up with another young adman he'd met while volunteering for the United War Work Campaign. By the 1940s, he was one of the industry's grand old men, ready to pass on the lessons he'd learned. His book *Your Creative Power* was published in 1948. An amalgam of pop science and business anecdote, it became a surprise bestseller. Osborn promised that by following his advice, the typical reader could double his creative output. Such a mental boost would spur career success and also make the reader a much happier person. "To get your foot in the door, your imagination can be an open-sesame," he wrote. "The more you rub your creative lamp, the more alive you feel."

Your Creative Power was filled with tricks and strategies, such as always carrying a notebook to be ready when inspiration struck. But Osborn's most celebrated idea was the one discussed in chapter 33, "How to Organize a Squad to Create Ideas." When a group works together, he wrote, the members should engage in a "brainstorm," which means "using the brain to storm a creative problem—and doing so in commando fashion, with each stormer attacking the same objective." For Osborn, brainstorming was central to BBDO's success. Osborn described, for instance, how the technique inspired a group of ten admen to come up with eighty-seven ideas for a new drugstore in ninety minutes, or nearly an idea per minute. The brainstorm had turned his employees into imagination machines.

The seven steps to effective brainstorming are:

1. Agree on the problem.
2. Gather the right team and the available data.
3. If possible, break down the problem.

4. Go for as many (quantity) ideas as possible.

5. Don't criticize as ideas are evaluated.

6. Combine several ideas to create an amazing new idea.

7. Fairly judge the created ideas for the best one that solves the problem.

The trouble with most brainstorming sessions is that participants only employ one of his steps correctly: the fourth step, ideation. The first step, however, is far more important because until you can define the problem at hand, all the methods to solve the problem are doomed to failure.

CREATE AN ENVIRONMENT FOR PROBLEM SOLVING

In earlier chapters I talked about how managers and entrepreneurs need to focus on solving real problems and not find themselves "selling" solutions that have nothing to do with the problem. In our Lavin Entrepreneurship Center at San Diego State University, if a student walks in and wants to meet with me to "pitch me an idea," the first question I have before we start is, "What problem are you solving?" In my Creativity and Innovation course, we spend the first four weeks of the semester learning how to identify and agree on problems before any brainstorming sessions start. It's a critical recognition, because we cannot brainstorm or come up with creative ideas until we agree on the problem. Learning how to identify real problems, not symptoms, is a critical skill. Here are four things you can do as a leader to create a company environment that is poised to solve problems:

1. **Encourage open communication.** Problem solving requires open communication where everyone's concerns and points

of view are freely expressed. I've seen too many times how difficult it is to get to the root of the matter in a timely manner when people do not speak up. Open communication is critical. That is why when those involved in the problem would rather not express themselves—fearing they may threaten their job and/or expose their own or someone else's wrongdoing—the problem-solving process becomes a "bad" treasure hunt. Effective communication toward problem solving happens because of a leader's ability to facilitate an open dialogue between people who trust their intentions. Only then will they feel that they are in a safe environment to share why they believe the problem happened as well as specific solutions.

2. **Break down walls.** Open communication requires you to break down "walls" and enable a boundary-less organization whose culture is focused on the betterment of a healthier whole. Organizational "walls" are the root cause of most workplace problems and the reason many of them never get resolved. This is why today's new workplace must embrace an entrepreneurial spirit where employees can freely navigate and cross-collaborate to connect the problem-solving dots. Breaking down walls allows a leader to more easily engage their employees to get their hands dirty and solve problems together.

3. **Hire and retain people with growth mindsets.** Breaking down walls and communication barriers requires people to have an open "growth" mindset. In the end, problem solving is about people working together to make the company serve the customer better. Therefore, if you are stuck working with people who are closed-minded, effective problem solving

can't even begin. People with growth mindsets see beyond the obvious details before them and view risk as their best friend. They tackle problems head-on and get on with the business of driving growth and innovation. Fixed-mindset employees turn things around to make it more about themselves and less about what is required to convert a problem into a new opportunity.

4. **Use problem solving as a way to bond.** Effective leaders who are comfortable with problem solving always know how to gather the right people, resources, budget, and knowledge from past experiences. They inspire people to lift their game by making the problem-solving process highly collaborative; for them, it's an opportunity to bring people closer together. I've always believed that you don't know the true potential and character of people until you see the way they solve problems.

SIMPLE DOS AND DON'TS OF BRAINSTORMING SESSIONS

Our agency had some of the most creative people in the world and we "solved" an amazing variety of problems for our clients. We used brainstorming almost every single day, from informal meetings to regular sessions. Here are some simple insights to the dos and don'ts of a brainstorming session:

Brainstorming Sessions Done Right

Bring together a diverse team. This is a critical element to building a team that can think "differently" in looking at the same problem. Mix people with varied backgrounds and skill sets to get better possible approaches to a solution. A football team can't win with eleven quarterbacks, so why would you put similar people on the same team?

Define and agree on the problem. When a team first comes together, share the "facts" on the problem and have the team thoroughly discuss and provide input as to the real cause of the problem. Employees who are taking sick days and missing work may be doing so because of health issues, not morale.

Discourage criticism but encourage wild ideas. The worst thing you can do in a brainstorming group is to critique or criticize initial ideas. Encourage open giving of ideas so that other people can react to a "creative" environment and share their "deep" ideas. Research into creativity and brainstorming sessions has shown that even in a good brainstorming environment, most participants still hold back 50 percent of their ideas for fear of being wrong.

Make quantity of ideas more important than quality. Brainstorming is one place where lots of ideas are good and quantity trumps quality. Why? Because a group of five people creating twenty-five ideas/solutions to evaluate is better than only evaluating five ideas or solutions. Also, you are more likely to combine or create ideas off each other when you have a high quantity. You suggest vitamins, I suggest water, and someone else suggests vitaminwater.

When energy fades, build on the best idea. This is another reason the quantity of ideas or solutions is so important.

Once you get to a place where the energy of the group fades, now you build on the best idea, which itself may end up being a combination of other ideas. Get the group focused now on designing and building the best solution.

Draw and sketch so that everyone can see the ideas. This is where you engage the right side of your brain. Drawing out the ideas allows people to process them with the "creative" side of their brain. This exercise will lead to even more creativity as people "see" what's in front of them and begin to add even more ideas, which hopefully they share with the group.

If possible, create 2-D and 3-D models. There is nothing like the real thing or a prototype to have people really understand the potential of a solution. If possible, use a 3-D printer to create a mock-up of a product solution or, if it's something larger, use Legos, Play-Doh, or construction paper to actually build a rough prototype of a possible solution. In my class, using Play-Doh students created a retail fashion store layout to appeal to millennials.

How to Kill Brainstorming Sessions

Brainstorming sessions done well can accomplish quite a bit and get amazing results, especially through group "think" and discussion. However, avoid these mistakes that will hurt or even seriously hinder brainstorming:

Having Senior Management Speak First, in Order of Importance: There is no better way to intimidate your team or employees than to have senior leaders speak first. Who is going to disagree or potentially disappoint them with a perceived weak or crazy idea? No one. Let everyone or anyone go first, even the intern. This person may spark a winning idea.

Having Everyone Go in Turn Around the Table: When you do this you limit the input of unique ideas because people get caught up in building on what they already heard or thinking they have to be "smart" on the spot when it's their turn next. Remove the pressure and gently involve all people by encouraging random and different ideas; encourage quantity and don't judge any ideas until you are at the end of the ideation part of brainstorming.

Bringing in Only "Look-alike" Team Member Experts: In my class, we have students from all over the campus and that is what builds diverse teams. If you have only business school students or computer science students you can almost predict weak and narrow results. Diversify your brainstorming team as much as possible.

Only Holding Brainstorm Sessions Off-Site: I have never understood this one. Let's take everyone from the company and move to a hotel conference room and come up with a new killer product. Really? This practice sends two messages that are both bad: First, we only brainstorm when we leave the building (not at work all the time?), and second, you need to be in a really noncreative room to come up with a breakthrough idea. Hold brainstorm meetings in different thought-provoking spaces, including outdoors.

Encouraging Professional Behavior, No Silly Stuff: Give your participants the freedom to be serious, silly, and in between.

Encourage playfulness with purpose: Start off the meeting with a drawing contest to visualize the problem or something that sparks the idea that there are no set rules to coming up with a creative solution. You can't force creativity. If you try, you will get only vanilla ideas—and not even French vanilla.

Having Everyone Take Copious Notes: When people take copious notes, two things happen and both are bad: First, people spend time taking detailed notes and not being creative, and second, no one is sharing notes in real time. Use a whiteboard and draw/write all ideas where everyone can see them, or use a cloud-sharing tool where all participants can "draw" on the same page and build on each other's ideas, sparking even more ideas.

Every Creative House Needs Structure

On the very first day of class, once attendance and the course overview is completed, I indicate I am disappointed with a certain product that I place on the table. I tell the students they need to solve my problem. Before they get into groups, I walk them through a brainstorming structure that they are to use every single time they get into brainstorming groups:

- **Five to Ten Minutes:** Take this time to agree on the real problem.
- **Ten Minutes:** Generate as many ideas/solutions as possible, twenty-five minimum.
- **Five to Ten Minutes:** Decide on the best idea or combination of ideas that best solves the problem.
- **Ten to Fifteen Minutes:** Draw, don't write out, the final solution.

You might think, what could ten random groups of students possibly come up with? I have to tell you, it's incredible. Maybe not on the first day, but over the next fifteen weeks they never cease to amaze me. Slowly, as they work their way through several brainstorming exercises, they begin to shift their mindset. Crazy and wild ideas are celebrated. Criticism is not allowed. Their drawings get more refined and creative. They develop their own culture, similar to a company. By week six, the students can't wait to come to class and see what challenges I will throw at them. I see the "growth mindset" begin to develop and accelerate. They are behaving like young children again just spewing ideas into the air. They are drawing and sketching like they have not since kindergarten. No coloring inside the lines here. By the tenth week, as we move into more complex challenges, they are on fire.

I bring several experts into the classroom and ask them to run structured brainstorming exercises around a big problem or brand challenge. They include founders of companies and creators of brands. The brainstorming exercises are run with the same structure, thirty to forty minutes maximum. We had a world-renowned product design expert challenge the class to create an affordable "luxury" product for the rising millennial target market. One expert challenged the class to create the world's smallest functional and personal office space. As the student groups presented their drawn solutions, he commented that two of the proposed solutions were impressive, viable, and possible commercial products. An action sports founder and brand expert challenged the class to create an action sports brand and product, from scratch, that solved a specific problem for a defined target audience. In about forty minutes, student groups came up with suggested products and logos, and as they presented their ideas via drawings, the expert commented that he felt there were several potential brands and products in the room.

One of the key elements in brainstorming is to have the moderator or a volunteer list every idea on a surface that everyone on the team can see and then draw the final solution. Why do I always make them draw it?

WHEN WE DRAW, CREATIVITY RULES THE BRAIN

In Chapter 1, I discussed the research and the debate about left-brain (analytical) versus right-brain (creative, visual) thinking when it comes to how people behave. Even though the recent research has concluded that we actually use regions of both halves of the brain when solving problems, the halves of the brain still have their core functional areas. Turns out that when you draw, you actually "quiet" the left side of the brain and really let the right side of the brain be more creative. If I ask you to print the word "box," your left brain will dominate the assignment. If I ask you to draw a box, your right brain will kick in. If I ask you to draw a colorful 3-D box with a horse on one side, you are really moving into right-brain mode. Another real benefit of drawing out solutions is that the entire team sees the drawing and comes up with even more creative ideas. Why? Their right brains are kicking in; the more they "see" the possible solutions, the less analytical they are and the more open and creative they become. It's not just a "belief" or a wish; their brains are reacting to visual and drawn stimuli. If you don't believe me, run your next brainstorming session in a structured time frame, thirty-five or forty minutes, and tell the participants that they cannot talk or take written notes. They have to draw everything, even the early ideas. Use sticky notes that can be placed on a large piece of cardboard or use a whiteboard. Watch what happens. A great by-product of this type of exercise, with no talking, is that there is no criticism of ideas. Plus people visually build on each other's ideas, drawing new ideas based on combinations of ideas they have just seen. Oh, the brain is firing now!

BRAINSTORMING THE RIGHT WAY: USING TOOLS

I have mentioned that brainstorming without structure can be a waste of time. You need the discipline of understanding the problem first and then, using a limited time frame, the aid of a brainstorming tool. Here are six tools:

1. **SCAMPER:** This is a great tool that has you analyzing a number of options when looking at a current problem (works well when analyzing a current product or service).
2. **IdeaGen:** This is a tool similar to mind-mapping where you start with a central problem and branch out to possible solutions.
3. **Phoenix List:** This is a tool created within and used by the Central Intelligence Agency (CIA) when tackling cold cases.
4. **Blue Ocean Strategy:** A purposeful framework, it is used to analyze your current position in a competitive marketplace (the red ocean) and to determine the "blue ocean" you should be in.
5. **Tempero:** This is a tool you can use to take several "pieces and parts" from existing solutions to create a new solution.
6. **Observation Lab:** This a great tool that has you really observing what you normally don't see, hear, smell, etc., in order to create customer-driven improvements.

After using these tools over the past four years at San Diego State University, I can attest that the creative results they produce have been amazing and I would not hold a brainstorming session without using one of them. In the upcoming chapters, I will thoroughly explain each brainstorming tool and give you several examples of real exercises we do as part of our course work.

In Chapter 8, I will provide you with a point of view and reference on why product or service "iteration" is actually the driver of innovation, more so than random innovation itself. Iteration is good. But so many managers and entrepreneurs I meet really don't look at the opportunity of iterating something better in the marketplace to better meet customers' needs. Rather, they "think" they need to come up with something "original" or something the world has never seen before. Not necessarily so. In fact, 95 percent or more of new products or services are iterations from existing products or services. It's not about your "epiphany" idea for a new startup that came to you in the middle of the night or while on a Ferris wheel; it's about gaps and unmet customer needs in big marketplaces.

CREATIVE / INNOVATIVE INSIGHT

This serial entrepreneur has a strong point of view on brainstorming your way to innovation. He actually hates the term "think outside of the box." His point of view is that everyone has to behave and think in creative and innovative ways every day. It has to be part of the culture. He believes it's hard to be creative unless you are in a creative environment. Spending more time on defining the problem succinctly is better than spending too much time on possible solutions. And make sure everyone is

(continued on next page)

(continued from previous page)

heard, even the "quiet" people. Add some diversity to your brainstorming group to get different points of view. It's also important to write or draw everything; capture it all and let it digest. As a leader, listen. But then critically follow through and implement the best idea(s). At times, you will need to make a decision based on gut or instinct. And that will involve some risk. To quote him: "You never know with these things when you're trying something new what can happen. This is all experimental." I don't know about you, but I would love to be in a brainstorming session with Richard Branson.

Key Takeaway

Using brainstorming tools effectively should spawn an amazing amount of creative ideas focused on solving a problem. However, you need to have innovation ingrained in your culture. People need to believe that in order to survive and grow to be a leader, innovation is not an option. It is actually required.

CHAPTER EIGHT

ITERATION AND INNOVATION ARE PERSONAL

If you were a product, how would you iterate yourself to be more innovative? Seriously, what simple "iterative" changes would you make to yourself so that you had the potential to be more innovative? Most people never look at themselves this way. Similarly, most people think that in order to be wildly successful in their career, they need to hit the proverbial "home run" all the time. That's almost statistically impossible.

In this chapter, let me give you a better approach to embracing iteration and innovation in your personal life; then you can use that mindset, knowledge, and perspective to create some real impact in your professional career, too.

THE SIMPLICITY OF ITERATION

Most of the world's new products and services come from iterations of existing products and services. Why? It's just easier to incrementally improve something we already know from our memory or that we can physically touch or see. It's really hard to come up with something totally new that the world has never seen before. So, in order to embrace fully the notion that iteration can lead to innovation, let's look at how you could bring the concept of iteration to yourself. You have limited resources and need to manage them effectively. Here are four powerful suggestions that if you adopt will "iterate" a more innovative you:

1. **Simplify your life.** You have limited resources (time, energy, money) and if you invest in fewer but more strategic life elements (commitments, goals, changes, etc.) you can get so much more focused. To do that, simplify or eliminate elements of your life. Here are a few suggestions: Watch less screens. Downsize your expenses. Do things in bulk (e.g., cook multiple meals at the same time or check email two or three times during the day rather than all the time). Don't work on weekends (refresh yourself). Learn to say no more often. . . . You see, productivity is not about doing more; it's about doing things well.

2. **Little things matter.** Just as with products or services, incremental changes are easier to get done. So, look at the key elements in your life and look at where you can make simple "iterative" changes. It's too hard to change yourself overnight (via a fad diet) or radically adjust your monthly budget. But it is easy to make a cup of coffee at home and not spend $4 daily for a cup of Starbucks; that $20 a week adds up to $1,040 a year. Make a few little changes that allow you to live simpler and with less clutter and expense.

3. **Be more curious.** Take stock of your professional life. Do you have an amazing mentor? If not, find one. Could you improve your network by adding people with different

backgrounds and perspectives? When was the last time you visited a place you don't usually go to (e.g., an art gallery)? Read articles and books on subjects that are trending. Try food that is presented in a different way. Go take a drawing class. Look at the things you do in your life that you enjoy and investigate them further.

4. **Get things done.** As you think about the previous suggestions, don't just ponder them—start doing them. Don't be someone that always talks about making changes but never seems to do them. If one of your goals is to run a marathon (big goal), do something small first: Get a subscription to *Runner's World* or buy a new pair of running shoes or perhaps go to a runners' meet up, all before you start running. Do something small and iterative to get going.

It's not always easy to make changes in our lives. But we are responsible for what we choose to do. So commit to making small iterative changes to your life that begin to shape a more innovative you.

PERSONAL INNOVATION

Hopefully, by now you realize that the notion that some people are just born to be more creative and innovative is just not true. You can intentionally affect your mindset and perspective with regard to innovation. Here are some simple but powerful perspectives on creating that more innovative you:

◆ The innovation switch is always on. Innovation is about approaching your daily work and the challenges you face with an open mind and a creative, can-do attitude. It's about seeking unconventional solutions to the problems on your plate. At work, it's looking at everything you do and figuring out where you can do better, in less time, with fewer motions, in a way that adds value to both internal and external customers. Instead of approaching a single task with the attitude, "Okay, now I've got to get creative," the innovator approaches everything in life with this attitude. Instead of looking at "being creative" as something you need to do consciously, see it as something you do unconsciously, like breathing.

♦ Innovation needs to add value. When the global economic crisis hit, everything changed. Four-dollar lattes suddenly became unaffordable luxuries. McDonald's attacked with McCafé. Dunkin' Donuts began serving premium coffee. Starbucks was forced to shutter 800 stores, lay off 5,000 employees, cut $500 million in costs, offer discounts, advertise, and look for even more ways to become efficient. Innovation is about more than innovating new products. It's understanding where you can add the most value where you are every day.

♦ Innovation is needed everywhere. Many times I've heard people make assumptions and say, "My company doesn't want me to be creative. They just want me to get my work done." The question isn't whether innovation is wanted and needed in your firm; it's where and when it's needed. Be curious when a senior employee or manager tells you why things are done the way they are. Certainly listen to that voice in your head when you see a better way of doing something. And then channel that big-picture, "opportunity-spotting" mindset right back into how you do your work.

♦ Walk the talk. Innovation is about taking action. Like all of us, you could have a good idea and just not follow through with it. And we are good at coming up with excuses. We can blame bureaucracy. We are good at convincing ourselves that innovating a new idea went "beyond our job description." We could turn the idea over to someone else to pursue. But here is what you need to do: Take action. Overcome the obstacles and get buy-in for a new idea and refuse to take "no" for an answer. *Do.*

SOMETHING OLD, SOMETHING NEW

By now, you are starting to understand that creativity, and possibly innovation, are directly related to having the right mindset, the right environment, and the right habitat. The word "innovation" might conjure up the thought that you have to have a breakthrough idea to be truly innovative. Wrong. You would be better served to have a mentality of believing that to successfully innovate is to be prepared to iterate like crazy. As Proust wrote, "The real voyage of discovery consists not in seeking new landscapes, but in having new eyes."

We have the mistaken belief that most of the things in the world we know must have been these amazing innovations. Not so. Apple did not create the world's first MP3 player when it launched the iPod. Google was not the world's first search engine (about twenty others were created before it). Facebook did not launch social media. Coca-Cola was not the world's first soft drink. McDonald's did not create the hamburger. Henry Ford did not create the world's first automobile. Is Netflix an innovation over Blockbuster? Probably not; perhaps only an evolution of an existing service to a new service. Why does all this talk of iteration versus innovation matter? And what does that have to do with creativity? Because you need to know that you can be creative and innovative by being iterative. Most of the world's new products or services are derivatives from other existing products or services. It's hard to create a breakthrough product or service without first examining the current products or services in the marketplace with your problem in mind. You can address a health and fitness problem with a new product from two existing products (fitness tracking + health monitoring = Fitbit). And if you are working on something revolutionary, which will involve innovation (let's say the Internet), you still need to study the problem from different perspectives. Vinton Gray "Vint" Cerf, one of the creators of the Internet, studied computer-to-computer communications and networking protocols for years before helping to "connect the dots" and create the leap from a government-based network backbone to what we now know as the Internet.

MAKE IT BETTER TO MAKE IT GREAT

Channeling T. S. Eliot's maxim "Good poets copy, great poets steal," Steve Jobs once said, "At Apple, we have always been shameless about stealing great ideas." Our marketing agency worked with Steve at NeXT, Pixar, and Apple and he did not mean "legally" steal. He meant that innovation is simply improving something previously invented, or taking small and powerful iterative steps to make something better.

It's not about copying. It's about purposely taking something to another level to better solve a problem. Look at how we have "iterated or evolved" the mobile phone into today's smartphone. While the first mobile phone was probably revolutionary, the phones following were iterations and maybe an evolution to smartphones today. If you start with an existing product or service and look to improve it in some small way, your iteration might be an innovation. Or better yet, a successful product or service.

THINK SMALL TO GET BIG

When thinking about creating something new or solving a big problem, start with an iteration mentality and perhaps you might create an innovative product or company. You should know that innovation has several stepping-stones. Let's examine the different spectrums of innovation: incremental (iterations), evolutionary, and revolutionary.

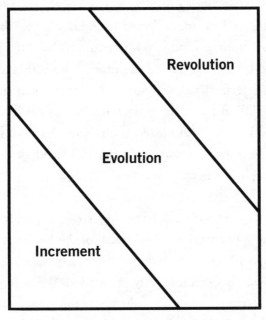

[SPECTRUMS OF INNOVATION]

Incremental innovation involves small but critical adjustments to existing services or products, and I feel like this is what we see the most of in today's marketplaces. These types of innovations, although small, still matter a lot. So please don't interpret incremental innovation as a substitute for bad to good or less meaningful to more meaningful. Iterative innovations are vital. They typically do not bring about a larger change in the marketplace. But they can be wildly successful with a specific target market. Examples are a Dropbox product (storage in the cloud versus on your hard drive) or perhaps Facebook, which by improving the interface of the social media platform, rocketed its way to become a dominant leader.

Evolutionary innovation can seem like a massive change. But, at its heart, the "new thing" is still strongly grounded in the "old thing." A little more dramatic and noticeable than iterative innovations, evolutionary innovations have the potential to lead to larger-scale changes. But, with hindsight, they tend to be an intermediary step along the way to something different. Think of LinkedIn replacing business cards or Netflix moving on from Blockbuster. Both examples involve a new medium and environment, although the product or service, at its core, is not new.

Revolutionary innovation, as one might deduce, truly involves something different that leaves much of the old behind. Using phones as an example, whatever replaces landline phones entirely will be a revolutionary innovation. When the first cell phone was created, it was a revolutionary innovation. You might say the first television, the first zipper, the first chainsaw, the first firearm, and the first sewing machine all were revolutionary innovations that sparked or exploded big marketplaces. What do you see or are curious about that you should investigate?

It's really hard to create a revolutionary product or service. They usually come about when someone has been studying a problem with an existing product or when faced with a big problem in a marketplace. How do we cut a forest down with an axe or a saw? Is there a faster way or better way? Chainsaw. Don't start with the notion that you have to create a revolutionary new product innovation. Instead, study a problem in a marketplace where the current products or services are falling short of their customers' expectations. Therein lies the opportunity.

IMITATION IS THE SINCEREST FORM OF FLATTERY

It may not sound sexy, but starting a new business or division that builds on an existing technology, product, or business model is usually less risky and smarter than introducing something that is completely disruptive and needs customer adoption. Can you afford to educate, nurture, and bring the customers along with you? Maybe, if you have $50 million. There are many levels of innovation that go beyond copying someone else's idea but stop short of pushing the bleeding edge.

Many of the major businesses that are around today started this way. McDonald's did not really invent the fast-food model; it simply improved on the cookie-cutter White Castle process. Starbucks did not invent the coffee café; it just improved on creating a friendly place that happens to have coffee. Apple did not invent portable media players, smartphones, or laptop computers; it just made them easier to use.

The advantage of imitation, with incremental innovation, is that it usually gives you a large existing customer base. It also allows you to take advantage of products or companies that have come before you so that you can perhaps move faster with less risk. Let's examine the advantages of incremental (iteration) innovation:

Eliminates Research and Development: If you can draw on observations, research, and other data from existing products, customers, competitors, and marketplaces, you don't need to do as much research to quantify a marketplace opportunity. For example, if you knew the pet food segment in the pet industry was stable, that there were 77 million dogs in the United States, and that healthy pet food trends were on the rise, it's not a stretch to simply deliver *organic* dog food to the marketplace.

Learns from Early Adopters and Competitors: Smart startups save cost and time by capitalizing on the pivots of others before them. Market research can thus be based on real customers and a previously tested market. Studying and learning from the mistakes of others is the best way to reduce your own risks. Facebook did this perfectly, learning from what Friendster and MySpace had done right and wrong to move more quickly into the social media marketplace.

Drives Progress Through Continuous Innovation: The computer industry and others have used this model for years, so business processes and metrics for innovation are well documented. Disruptive technologies are random and their success is unpredictable. Good imitators, such as McDonald's, often bypass the original innovator. As an aside, I worked with Amazon in the early days and it was not the first online bookseller. Who was? Who cares.

Looks to Related Markets or Another Country: The world is now an increasingly small place, and startups or new product divisions usually don't have the resources to saturate all of the markets at once. Imitation with innovation is a great way to jump ahead of the curve. Timing is critical, as is a focus on marketing and meeting customer needs. Remember, competitors can also move quickly, and there may not be intellectual property (IP) to protect you. Amazingly, many startups outside the USA look to Silicon Valley and then quickly create their equivalent of a successful company (e.g., Amazon, eBay, Facebook, Yahoo!, Airbnb, or even a new retail product or service) in their own regional markets.

SET YOUR INNOVATION SIGHTS ON MARKETPLACES

People pitch me ideas all the time. In my role as director at the Lavin Entrepreneurship Center, I listen to pitches from students and local entrepreneurs and get to hear lots of interesting ideas. But let's assume you are a would-be entrepreneur but you don't have an amazing idea for a startup. Or you are a product marketing specialist struggling to come up with a new product. Here is a thought. Rather than straining to come up with an "innovative idea," examine a large and/or growing marketplace thoroughly; get to know its workings so well that you might well surface a problem or opportunity. Only then should you try to create that new product or service. Sound backward? I don't think so. Let's look at what has happened to the "taxi service/car rental" marketplace in the past fifteen or so years. What was the core customer problem? One, people needed to get somewhere. Secondary problem: They don't like the service from taxis. However, the only solution in the marketplace was to either rent a car (expensive) or take a taxi. Zipcar was founded in June 2000 to solve that problem. Car rental whenever you need it, by the hour, in your local town. Here comes the competition in 2008 with Car2Go. Similar service with a few "iterative" twists. Let's say you are looking at this growing marketplace but you don't have the money to buy a fleet of cars to start your business. What do you do? In our class, we would have had a creative brainstorming session and we would have created an "evolutionary" solution, driven by our lack of funding. What would we have created to solve the problem of getting someone from A to B a little bit easier and better? Uber.

I am a big fan of large, emerging, or disrupted marketplaces. The notion that people just need to come up with new ideas to create a successful company may work sometimes, but I have learned that it's the marketplace that matters most. You can have an amazing idea, but if there is no clear market opportunity, it might just as well be worthless. So, a better way to look at product or service innovation is to start with the marketplace, then follow with the idea, which usually is a solution to a problem customers are having.

If you are looking for innovative ideas for new products and services, consider them in the context of their marketplace. So, if you generate some creative ideas and you take your best idea and it's a potentially great product or service, put that idea into the marketplace. But ask yourself these simple questions first:

- Does my idea solve a problem in the marketplace?
- Can I easily test my idea in the marketplace?
- Is the market easily defined?
- Can I reach people in the marketplace easily?
- Is the market growing?
- Does the leader in the market offer this idea?
- Will customers value my idea?

- Is the marketplace being disrupted?
- Is the marketplace fragmented?

With the CreativityWorks Framework in mind, examine some growing marketplaces, take the best one, and either target a favorable market or come up with a low-risk strategy in a potentially unfavorable market. You really can't put together a product innovation and implementation strategy unless you understand the marketplace and its potential customers. The more you examine that potential marketplace, the more you will learn. Remember, you don't "need" to create an original, unique solution to create an amazing product or company. You just need to solve a real problem or better meet a customer need.

The next six chapters are shorter and to the point and highlight the six brainstorming tools I use in my Creativity and Innovation course. By the way, I use the same brainstorming tools with the twenty or so business founders I mentor whenever they need to drive some creative solutions or solve a problem. I do eat my own dog food.

CREATIVE / INNOVATIVE INSIGHT

Simple iteration seems simple but can be powerful. In 2010, I was teaching an entrepreneurship course where student teams had to come up with an idea for a product they could validate during the rest of the semester. One student team pitched their idea of creating a macronutrient- and protein-packed shake. I said, "No, sounds like Juice It Up! or Jamba Juice." I told them to come up

(continued on next page)

(continued from previous page)

with something else. They came back the next week and pitched me the same idea. But this time they provided me some insight into the competition's products, which had too much sugar and not enough fresh ingredients. They indicated their shake would have no sugar and only natural and fresh ingredients with a high amount of protein. Their plan was to sell it inside or just outside of fitness locations, similar to a large fitness facility we had on campus. I approved the project. They did a good job on their project but surprised me when they said they would like to launch a startup around the product idea. I told them I was not sure that their product was "different" enough to be embraced by the marketplace. I was wrong. Today, they operate nine locations and will do more than $3 million in revenue. They "iterated" a better product and delivered it to an existing marketplace but to a new target segment, the rapidly growing eighteen- to thirty-five-year-old millennials. Booyah.

Key Takeaway

If you know your target segment and test your marketplace, your product or service does not have to be evolutionary or revolutionary. It can be a simple iteration of an existing product or service; one that is very important to your customer and that alone can create an amazing product or company.

CHAPTER NINE

PHOENIX LIST:
CIA TOOL FOR EVERYONE

The key to understanding a potential problem is learning how to ask the right questions. A great tool for this is the Phoenix List, a list of questions the CIA developed to help with tough or cold cases. It's useful when looking at a current opportunity where iteration or innovation is needed but you or the team are stumped. Let's start at the beginning: What is the problem?

THE WORLD LOVES PROBLEMS

Simple and smart questions define problems well and lead to a clear vision of the issues involved. When that occurs, it's easier to run multiple scenarios to their conclusion and find the best solution to the problem.

Here are four insights that will have you asking better questions:

1. **Questions help people discern.** Dolphins use sonar to "see" in murky or dark water. They send out a click sound and wait for the echo to return. Once they have enough echo responses, they can navigate, find prey, and avoid obstacles and predators. Questions are the business equivalent of sonar. Asking the right question will help you find your way through a problem, locate the right customers, avoid future difficulties, and outperform your competitors. Questions also act as a filter that will help you decipher the key elements of a problem.

2. **Deep assessment is necessary.** To reach a solution, finding answers to the "What?" (What is broken . . . is working . . . needs improvement . . . must be changed . . . will have the biggest impact?) and the "Why?" (Why did this happen . . . are our customers considering the competition . . . are we losing this market . . . are we using this process . . . is our product third instead of first?) is critical. Questions such as these matter. Asking a series of clear questions leads to precision. When questions are developed with this result in mind, they will generate a natural sorting and sifting during the discovery process.

3. **Frame your questions in layers.** Unfortunately, most people don't take the time to frame the questions beforehand or to ask questions in layers. Effective questions are powerful and thought provoking. They are open ended and not leading. They are more often "What?" or "How?" questions. Although "Why?" questions are good for soliciting information, they can make people defensive—so be thoughtful in your use of them. Also, to be an effective questioner, wait for the answer—don't provide it yourself.

4. **Understand the problem together.** When working with other people to solve a problem, it's not enough to describe the problem to them; they need to understand it for themselves. You can help them do this by asking questions that lead them to think about the topic. A great opener to any new project is: "What do you think is the problem?" Behind effective questioning lies the ability to listen to the answer and suspend judgment. This means being intent on understanding what the person is really saying. What is behind his or her words? Fear? Excitement? Resistance? Let go of your preconceptions so they don't block you from learning more information. Gather the facts and then pay attention to your gut for additional data.

When you ask smart, simple questions, you will connect with people in a more meaningful way, understand the problem with greater depth, defuse volatile situations, get cooperation, seed your own ideas, and persuade people to work with you because you've gained their confidence. Most important, you will be able to work through and discard a series of possible solutions that will lead you to the one best scenario that you'll implement. Using this method, you'll increase the likelihood of developing the right answer to the problem—and increase your knowledge base at the same time.

THE PHOENIX LIST: QUESTIONS MATTER

When solving a problem, lots of people are taught to research the problem and analyze the data. But the missing piece is the "thinking" part. And that needs to happen regularly from beginning to end in order to understand the system involved and how the parts work together. That's why I love the CIA's Phoenix List.

Research without thinking only takes us to obvious places. We don't see connections because we don't look for them; instead, we're only seeing connections from others' research and opinions. We're only seeing what presents itself, which is just data. In the end, we're left with no insights about the problem we're solving, but only a catalog of facts that are pretty obvious to both ourselves and everyone else.

The Phoenix List of questions was developed by the CIA to encourage agents to look at a challenge from different angles regardless of any inhibiting contexts, essentially creating multiple thought experiments for us to logically and systematically navigate the problem, giving us a much fuller understanding. And with a fuller understanding of the problem comes more energy spent on highly relevant solutions. When presented with a challenge, knowing what to ask is the difference between doing more of the same and doing something extraordinary.

Using the Phoenix List is like holding your challenge in your hand. You can turn it, look at it from underneath, see it from one view, hold it up to a different position, and imagine solutions.

It's very easy to get started. Just follow this process:

1. **Write your challenge to the problem.** Isolate the challenge you're thinking about and commit yourself to an answer by a certain date.
2. **Ask the questions.** Use the Phoenix List of questions to dissect the challenge into as many different parts as you can.
3. **Record and draw your answers.** Don't be judgmental or critical; record every answer to the questions and draw out problems and answers when you can.

The Phoenix List Questions

First, you use the "Problem" questions to really identify the problem and possible solutions; then you use the "Plan" questions to help you refine the solution you intend to implement. Here are the questions:

THE PROBLEM

- Why is it necessary to solve the problem?
- What benefits will you receive by solving the problem?
- What is the unknown?
- What is it you don't yet understand?
- What is the information you have?
- What isn't the problem?
- Is the information sufficient? Or is it insufficient? Or redundant? Or contradictory?
- Should you draw a diagram of the problem?
- Where are the boundaries of the problem?
- Can you separate the various parts of the problem? Can you write them down? What are the relationships of the parts of the problem? What are the constants of the problem?
- Have you seen this problem before?
- Have you seen this problem in a slightly different form? Do you know a related problem?
- Can you think of a familiar problem having the same or a similar unknown?
- Suppose you find a problem related to yours that has already been solved. Can you use it? Can you use its method?
- Can you restate your problem? How many different ways can you restate it? More general? More specific? Can the rules be changed?

♦ What are the best, worst, and most probable cases you can imagine?

THE PLAN

♦ Can you solve the whole problem? Part of the problem?

♦ What would you like the resolution to be? Can you picture it?

♦ How much of the unknown can you determine?

♦ Can you derive something useful from the information you have?

♦ Have you used all the information?

♦ Have you taken into account all essential notions in the problem?

♦ Can you separate the steps in the problem-solving process? Can you determine the correctness of each step?

♦ What creative-thinking techniques can you use to generate ideas? How many different techniques?

♦ Can you see the result? How many different kinds of results can you see?

♦ How many different ways have you tried to solve the problem?

♦ What have others done?

♦ Can you intuit the solution? Can you check the result?

♦ What should be done? How should it be done?

♦ Where should it be done?

♦ When should it be done?

♦ Who should do it?

♦ What do you need to do at this time?

♦ Who will be responsible for what?

♦ Can you use this problem to solve some other problem?

- What is the unique set of qualities that makes this problem what it is and unlike any other problem?
- What milestones can best mark your progress?
- How will you know when you are successful?

A Phoenix List Exercise

In my course, we always use a brainstorming tool to solve a problem in almost every class. We always use the same brainstorming structure to solve the problem. Here is an example I gave my students, and I'd like for you to solve the problem alongside them:

"I just came from the Barnes & Noble CEO's office," I say. "The CEO wants a solution to the declining revenue facing B&N. Oh, and he does not want to close any stores. You have about forty-five minutes to solve the problem."

First, the students, in groups of three to four, spend ten to twenty minutes using Phoenix List questions, and perhaps some simple marketplace research, to address and clarify the problem.

Next, they spend ten to fifteen minutes identifying possible solutions, as many as possible.

Then they spend ten minutes narrowing it down to the best solution(s).

Then they spend ten minutes drawing their best solution, which is then presented in front of the class. With forty-five or so students, that's about ten to twelve groups, each with their own idea.

Here is the scenario of how you would ask and potentially answer the Phoenix List questions to get at the core problem. The current definition of the problem is declining revenue.

- **Why is it necessary to solve the problem?** If we don't, the company fails.
- **What is the unknown?** The future mix of ebooks versus printed books.
- **Can you derive something useful from the information you have?** Self-published and photo book sales are rapidly rising, more than $5 billion combined since 2008.
- **What isn't the problem?** Revenue in the industry is still significant; 2008–2018 revenue will be flat ($15 billion) split between print and ebooks (ebooks rising, print books falling from $15 billion in 2008).
- **Have you seen this problem before?** Yes. Borders bookstores had this same problem; it did not change its business model and it failed.
- **Can you restate your problem?** Yes. Instead of focusing just on sales revenue, how can we change our business model to acquire more customers?

If you keep working your way through the questions, then the plan, you might end up where one of the student teams did in my classroom. In less than one hour, they came up with a potential solution to solve the sales revenue problem and keep 650 B&N stores afloat and growing. They identified what they thought the real problem was and their top recommendations on what to do next:

Real Problem:

The business model for B&N is broken.

Recommendations to Solve the Problem:

- Reduce the size of the printed books space in each store by 50 percent.

- Add a new "self-published" author "store within a store" area for writing workshops and editing and printing services, all generating new revenue.
- Sell local bestsellers through a new local author social media community marketing platform; authors will self-promote their new books.
- Add a new "create your photo book" area in the store where B&N staff can help customers create their photo books on the spot.

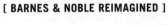

[BARNES & NOBLE REIMAGINED]

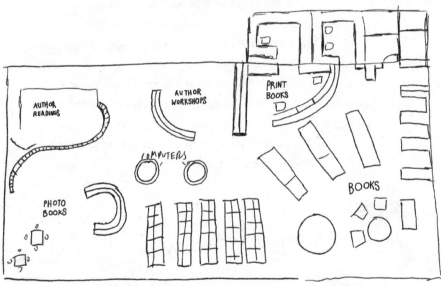

Look, I know what you are thinking. A student group on a university campus, even with a creative mindset, a great environment, and an amazing habitat, could not possibly come up with a potential solution to Barnes & Noble's problem in the marketplace. But they did. In less than one hour. I have been doing brand and integrated marketing for over twenty years and their recommendations are stunningly logical and insightful.

CREATIVE / INNOVATIVE **INSIGHT**

This company, once a fast-rising innovator, had lost its way. Revenue was still growing but its products were becoming "me too" in spite of their high prices. Leadership change was a constant as senior executives came and went. Engineers and product marketing spun out of control and delivered more products to the marketplace to keep the "quarterly" revenue engine running full out. You could almost "feel" the company's mojo seeping out of its products, employees, and even the buildings. What was the problem? Everyone seemed to have answers but no one seemed to have a strategy or a solution. In desperation, the company's board brought back one of the founders. Finding the company at the edge of bankruptcy, the founder decided the company would concentrate on just four product lines and declared that "innovation" and "delighting the customer again" was the focus, not revenue or profitability. The very next product was a major hit. Steve Jobs was back at Apple.

Key Takeaway

If you work in a company or are leading one, investigate and understand the difference between a symptom and a problem. It's critical to question everything until you arrive at the core problem. Then empower people to solve the problem.

10

IDEAGEN:
MAP YOUR SOLUTION

In the 1970s, researcher and educator Tony Buzan formally developed the idea behind mind mapping. The map's colorful, spider- or tree-like shape branches out to show relationships, solve problems creatively, and help you remember what you've learned. This chapter walks you through what a mind map is, explains how to construct and use it, showcases the benefits, and gives you an example of a live exercise I use in my Creativity and Innovation course.

It's hard to randomly generate good ideas unless they are connected to a central thought. That is the power of a mind map. Mind mapping is a visual form of note taking that offers an overview of a problem and its complex information, allowing you to comprehend ideas, create new ones, and build connections. Through the use of colors, images, and words, mind mapping encourages you to begin with a central problem and expand outward to more in-depth subtopics. Eventually, as you branch out, you can begin to identify solutions to the core problem at the outer ends of the branches.

Let's look at a simple but frustrating problem we all have probably experienced in order to help you better understand the concept of a mind map. The problem: plane flights being late. First, imagine an airplane flying in the sky. When you visualize or see an airplane in the sky, the airplane is your central focus at that moment. But your brain isn't done there. It also immediately begins to make references, or associations, to the airplane. These associations might include the color of the sky, different types of planes, how they fly, pilots, passengers, airports, and so forth. Because we think in images, not words, these associations often appear in a visual form in our minds. Your mind instantly starts making a map, creating links between these associations or concepts—a mental sort of spiderweb.

Now, think about planes arriving and taking off late. Why are they late? In order to understand the problem, you have to list all the major associations with the problem using main branches and then subbranches. Visualize a spiderweb or a tree full of branches now. With a mind map, you take the concept of the airplane and write *AIRPLANE* in the center (the spider's body or the trunk of the tree) of a horizontally oriented, blank piece of paper. Then, radiating out from the airplane are different-colored "main" lines (tree limbs or spider legs). On these you write the associations you had with airplanes, such as *PILOTS* and *AIRPORT*. From each of these are more associations, which you note on individual lines. In association with pilots you might think of their pay or training or even their stress. And so the mind map grows—(see Solving Late Plane Flights). Until you get to the ends of the branches or the web and begin to look at solutions to the problem for that branch.

[SOLVING LATE PLANE FLIGHTS]

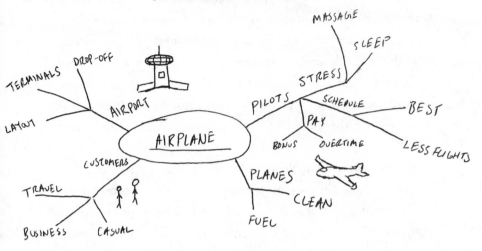

For example, with pilots, we can look at scheduling or high levels of stress and begin to suggest possible solutions, such as dynamic scheduling or massage therapy between flights. The great thing about a mind map like this one is that the entire team is creating it all on one page at the same time. So people build on each other's ideas in a visual way. That spawns other ideas or branches. Which leads to new potential solutions to the problem.

THE BRANCHES ARE GREATER THAN THE TREE

The benefits of using IdeaGen mind mapping are many. While brainstorming teams may not recognize the benefits immediately, once the core problem goes down in the center, then major attributes related to the core problem are identified and the "idea branches" and sketches start to flow. Let's look at the benefits:

Use your brain the way it thinks. When our brains lock onto something—an idea, sound, image, emotion, etc.—that "something" stands at the center of our thinking. Radiating out from it are countless other ideas, images, emotions, etc., that our brains associate with it. A mind map encourages radiant thinking by manifesting connections between and among these different pieces of information and concepts. And the more connections or associations our brains make to a thing, the more likely we are to remember it and use it.

Create and communicate information rapidly. Making these connections allows you to create and communicate information rapidly. As Randy L. Buckner and his associates noted in their 2008 Harvard University study, "The Brain's Default Network," writing and imagery both improve memory, creativity, and cognitive processing, and color is also a potent memory enhancer.

Map your way to "seeing" the problem. As humans we constantly create and devise approaches for solving problems. Doing so requires brainstorming. For instance, whether your concern is your wedding, new recipes, an advertising campaign, proposing a raise to your boss, better managing your money, a health diagnosis, or an interpersonal conflict, all can be mind-mapped. Mind maps are tools to capture information that's directly relevant to a problem, so you can compress large amounts of information quickly and easily.

Easily consume information and then use it. A mind map can order a complex process or system such as stock trades, computer networks, or engine mechanics.

Easily picture solutions. Finally, mind maps are useful in planning and executing potential solutions to problems. Adding small images and drawing out other iconic representations drive even more creativity. It is also a great visual tool for communicating the actual problem and potential solutions.

IDENTIFY THE PROBLEM AND THEN . . . EXERCISE

Let me walk you through another example of an exercise I use in my classroom so that you better understand the structure of using mind mapping in a brainstorming meeting. Imagine you are a student in my classroom and this is what happened when I walked into class one day:

"Our company has grown rapidly and we are now over 500 employees," I said. "But HR has noticed people are starting to miss work due to sick days. What is the problem and potential solution? You have forty minutes to come up with some solutions to the problem."

First, the students, in groups of three or four, spent five to ten minutes agreeing on the core of the problem; in this instance they determined the core problem of the employees to be their overall "health."

Next, they spent ten to fifteen minutes brainstorming using a mind map. They drew the core branches and then as many subbranches as possible, roughly sketching ideas and throwing down words on a poster-size piece of paper.

Then they spent ten minutes coming up with solutions to problems at the end of their branches.

Then they spent ten minutes refining their mind map, which was then presented in front of the class.

This is the best map they created around the core problem of "health":

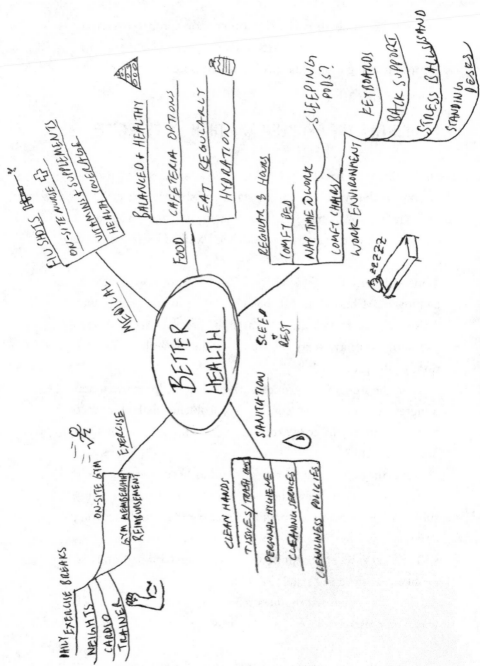

Map Features:

- Core branches of sleep and rest, food, sanitation, medical, and exercise
- Subbranches relating to main branches that further defined the problem
- Potential solutions such as nap time at work, an on-site nurse, daily exercise breaks, and balanced and healthy cafeteria options

You can see by the mind map that the core problem the students identified was not "too many sick days." Instead, they saw a high number of sick days as a symptom of other potential problems. You can see why proper identification and agreement of the problem is critical.

CREATIVE / INNOVATIVE INSIGHT

This entrepreneur started life in Europe and moved around several times before settling in London. He started playing with programming code and was fascinated with several application platforms, including social media and smartphones. He was curious about how and why people did what they do on these platforms and what kind of problems they encountered. He built several applications and tested them. Some gave him insight; others tried to solve a problem. He watched what people did when using their applications—and what they "consumed." He noticed a problem. He designed an

(continued on next page)

(continued from previous page)

application to solve the problem. He got a lot of downloads. A venture investor contacted him and offered an investment to take the application to another level. He took the money and pulled together an amazing team, including a scientist and several developers. Two years later, Yahoo! bought the company for $30 million. The entrepreneur was Nick D'Aloisio, who was just seventeen years old.

Key Takeaway

Be curious about what people "consume," no matter the product or service. Look for problems. Above all, if you get the chance to build a great team, build one that scares you personally. You don't have to be the smartest person on the team; just be the best leader.

CHAPTER ELEVEN

SCAMPER YOUR WAY TO INNOVATION

One of the most amazing brainstorming tools I have ever come across is called SCAMPER. It helps you look at something that exists today in a new light so that you can actually create what's needed tomorrow. The reason the students love it is that they don't "have to be creative" on the spot; they just have to analyze the product or service against the SCAMPER questions.

Let's look at the origin of SCAMPER; then I'll walk you through the questions, give you a few examples for today's marketplaces, and take you through a SCAMPER exercise from my course.

THE ORIGIN AND USE OF SCAMPER

One of the techniques that Alex Osborn liked to employ in his late-career brainstorming sessions was asking SCAMPER questions. He had observed that most new innovations were changes to something that already existed. Innovation does not have to be a radical departure from existing products or services. Often substantial improvements can be achieved with very subtle changes.

Bob Eberle then developed the mnemonic to organize Osborn's questions. The acronym stands for (S)ubstitute, (C)ombine, (A)dapt, (M)aximize or minimize, (P)ut to other uses, (E)liminate, and (R)earrange or reverse.

- **Substitute:** What elements of this product or service can we substitute?
- **Combine:** How can we combine this product/service with other products or services?
- **Adapt:** What idea from elsewhere can we alter or adapt?
- **Maximize or Minimize:** How can we greatly enlarge or greatly reduce any component?
- **Put to Other Uses:** What completely different use can we have for our product?
- **Eliminate:** What elements of the product or service can be eliminated?
- **Rearrange or Reverse:** How can we rearrange the product or reverse the process?

New niches, new products, and new markets can often be found by applying SCAMPER questions to existing products, even in mature industries. The process starts with a simple question; for instance: "How do we create a new product using the expertise that we already have?" Here are some simple examples of existing products or services using the SCAMPER method of brainstorming:

If you were making eyeglasses, then you could **substitute** plastic lenses for glass (incremental innovation) or you could substitute contact lenses for spectacles (radical innovation). A cell phone was **combined** with a camera and then an MP3 player. The roll-on deodorant was an idea **adapted** from the ballpoint pen. Restaurants that offer all you can eat have **maximized** their proposition. A low-cost airline like Ryanair in Europe has **minimized** (or eliminated) many elements of service. De Beers put industrial diamonds to **other use** when it launched engagement rings. Dell Computers and Amazon **eliminated** the intermediary distributor or retailer and sold directly to the consumer. And McDonald's **rearranged** the restaurant by getting customers to pay first and then eat.

How Each Element of SCAMPER Works

Substitute: The first letter in *SCAMPER, S,* for substitute, has you first examining the current product or service, breaking it into subcomponents, and then seeing what could actually be "substituted" to make the product better or unique for the target audience. Are there any components of the product that can be substituted or replaced with something else? In many industries the components that make up the products that are sold are numerous and so substitution is a very straightforward approach to innovation. For example, lightweight plastic parts substitute for metal components and solid-state electronics substitute for tubes and resistors. In the soft drink industry the introduction of artificial sweeteners created a whole new category of beverages—diet soda. Ford is substituting a lot of the steel in its F-150 pickup truck with lighter-weight aluminum to improve fuel economy.

Combine: When you look at the second letter in *SCAMPER, C,* for combine, you are looking to see what you could combine with the product or service to make it better or to perhaps create a new product. Our everyday life is full of examples of combined innovations. A cell phone includes a camera, an MP3 player, and GPS receiver, for example. Vitamin water is even more obvious a combination. Look around you, perhaps at your desk. What could be combined? A lamp with a stapler in its base? A stapler with a tape dispenser on top of it? A monitor with a light under the bottom edge?

Here's another brainstorming assignment I use in class: Examine nine existing products, then choose two and break both products down into their key components. Using the list of subcomponents, modify one of the current products or create an entirely new product. All in less than forty minutes.

Adapt: The third letter in *SCAMPER, A,* for adapt, has you examining other products or services from a point of view of what could be adapted to make your product or service better. Are there ideas from other industries that we can borrow and apply to the product? Carpenters borrowed the band saw from the meat-packing industry, banks lifted the ATM from the vending industry, and the electric car industry has begun to adapt laptop batteries as an energy storage medium. In another class exercise, students adapted the energy-producing power of a hand-cranked radio to a mountain bike that when pedaled provided an energy heat source to the handlebars—a perfect solution to cold hands in the winter.

Maximize or Minimize: The fourth letter in *SCAMPER, M,* for minimize or maximize, has you studying the existing product or service to see what you could minimize or maximize to make the product better. Are there components of the product that can be enlarged or shrunken? The obvious expression of this approach has been the miniaturization of electronics. But an equal number of innovations have been created by "maximizing" the size or portion of a product sold. Many of the innovations in the drink industry have come about by minimizing or maximizing the drink "size." Today it is possible to walk into the supermarket and buy a beverage in a 1-liter bottle; a 2-liter bottle; 6, 12, or 24 packs of 12-ounce cans; and even a single-serving 7.5-ounce "half-can." Each unique size of product has a unique demographic appeal and allows the manufacturer to sell to different consumers in a way in which manufacturers could not have previously. Another example of miniaturization might be the new digital smartwatches, like Apple Watch and others, which place a small computer on your wrist.

Put to Other Uses: The fifth letter of *SCAMPER, P,* for put to other uses, has you examining the current product and asking yourself, What else can this product, or elements of the product, do? Are there completely different uses for this product? Some manufacturers have figured out that there are multiple uses and have built advertising campaigns around these "nontraditional" uses. WD-40 and Duck brand duct tape have websites devoted to the myriad other uses for their products. There are IKEA hacks that show how to transform pieces of IKEA furniture into other pieces of furniture. One of the large beer manufacturers has sponsored a cook-off for recipes that use its product as an ingredient. Airbnb hosts put their spare bedrooms to another use each time they host an out-of-town guest. GORE-TEX, a waterproof technology, was originally used for years just for outerwear ski jackets. Now, you can also find GORE-TEX-treated gloves, socks, and footwear.

Eliminate: The sixth letter in *SCAMPER, E,* for eliminate, has you studying your product or service and saying, What makes the product better through elimination? Are there components or features of the product that can be eliminated? As devices have become more complex, opportunities are created in simplification. Some consumers only want their cell phone to send and receive calls, like the Jitterbug for seniors. Starbucks introduced a new juice line, Evolution Fresh, which uses a unique pasteurization process and eliminates preservatives for the health-conscious consumer market. Tablet computers eliminated the use of a keyboard. Wireless headphones and cordless phones eliminate, well, wires and cords.

Rearrange or Reverse: The final letter in *SCAMPER, R,* for rearrange or reverse, has you looking at your product or service and asking, What could be rearranged or reversed to improve the product or service? Is there an opportunity to rearrange the process? Often we assume that the way in which something is done is the only or best way to accomplish the task. Whole industries have been created by companies that were willing to experiment with the assumed or entrenched method of production. Uber and Lyft have rearranged how people look for a taxi—they don't; they just hail a ride from their app! Amazon has rearranged traditional retail sales channels by selling directly to the consumer and having us pay in advance and wait for the product to arrive (and sometimes even pay ahead for products on order).

Even in a flourishing economy there is always room for improvements to just about every product or service that is sold. The successful entrepreneur or product marketer is the one who can identify the need and provide an innovative idea to the marketplace. And the key to having a good idea is to have lots of them. Use SCAMPER to help you solve a problem or perhaps create a new product or service. Remember, when you use SCAMPER with a team of people, involve everyone and maximize your brainstorming session by drawing out the ideas for everyone to see. It just creates more "sparks."

To SCAMPER Is to Draw

No matter how you define it, a creative idea is nothing more than an idea—a thought in your head. Taking your ideas and making them into something more than just thoughts can be a daunting task for some people, but in actuality, making your ideas a reality is as easy as drawing them out. I have mentioned before that no matter the problem or exercise, the students in my courses draw their solutions. Oh, they can take notes, but they cannot make a recommendation or submit a final idea unless it is drawn. In addition to the whole "right versus left brain debate," you are definitely using your right brain more when you draw, so creativity is more apt to flow. Drawing out your ideas isn't just the first step to making your ideas real; there are a lot of things it can do for you and, more important, the others on your team. Here are several key benefits to drawing your ideas or solutions when brainstorming:

> **Drawing will help you visualize your thoughts.** Visual thinking genius (and author) Dan Roam once said: "By drawing . . . we will see otherwise invisible aspects and potential solutions [to problems that will] emerge." As human beings, we're visual creatures, and until you can visually see your ideas in front of you, you won't be able to accurately see potential problems (and solutions). Nor will others.

Drawing will inspire you and others. When you start to sketch out your ideas, the lines and shapes that start to form on the paper will help your mind visualize connections that can form new ideas. Your team members cannot share ideas they cannot see; drawing allows them to build off of something they all see. And that is where the potential magic will happen.

Drawing offers you the freedom to explore alternative ideas. Early in a project it's important to see a variety of different ideas so that you can choose the best option. Sketching lets you explore those varied ideas quickly. When you're sketching, your mind is free to play and explore other directions that surface. Sketches help filter out "rabbit hole" ideas—concepts that are impossible to produce or impractical to deliver on. Drawing out ideas works as an early-detection system— revealing potential issues before significant time is invested.

Drawing can foster discussions about ideas. With colleagues and especially clients, I've found sketches give everyone involved the permission to consider, talk about, and challenge the ideas they represent. After all, it's just a drawing. Because drawings are unfinished and loose, they invite commentary. There is latitude inherent in a sketch that seems to magically open the door for others to offer ideas—often thoughts you couldn't come up with from your singular perspective.

Drawing will get you organized. Ideas often seem simple and easy when they're in your head, but when you start getting those ideas onto paper they can seem overwhelming. Drawing your ideas—and all of the aspects of those ideas—on paper makes it easier for you to organize them. Even if your sketches are all over the place and not drawn in a Picasso fashion, just having something you can physically touch and see will get you organized.

Drawing your ideas means you can visualize them, rather than just imagine them. You can also organize your ideas and be inspired by drawing. For your next brainstorming session, use SCAMPER and invite everyone to draw out his or her ideas and solutions. Then build on what you all see and create something that solves the problem.

SCAMPER in the Classroom and Beyond

Here is an example from one of my classes during the 2013 semester of the Creativity and Innovation course:

> I walked into the classroom and said: "I don't like my sunglasses anymore. I need them to solve more problems I have in my life than just keeping the sun off my eyes. You have forty minutes to solve my problem."
>
> First, the students, in groups of three to four, spent five to ten minutes agreeing on the core of the problem. (In an exercise like this, I may give them a target segment—say, active people, age 22–35, who love technology.)
>
> Next, they spent ten to fifteen minutes brainstorming by drawing as many ideas as possible, roughly sketching ideas and throwing down words on a poster-size piece of paper.
>
> Then they spent ten minutes narrowing it down to the best idea(s).
>
> Then they spent ten minutes drawing their best idea, which was then presented in front of the class.
>
> The best idea that was drawn featured the following:

- Video camera in center
- Music player
- USB drive
- Bluetooth
- Interchangeable lenses
- GPS (panic alert)

In early 2016, I went online and found a pair of sunglasses that were being manufactured with some of the attributes I've just listed. (That not does mean they are or will be successful in the marketplace.)

[SUNGLASS DESIGN VIA SCAMPER]

This sketch was drawn by the team of students in 2013 as a result of a forty-minute brainstorming session. That's how early you can be in the game using SCAMPER.

CREATIVE / INNOVATIVE INSIGHT

This founder used product iteration as his core philosophy to move into the marketplace fast and get core traction; he would focus on product innovation later. The founder stumbled on his idea for a product when he was traveling. He tried to solve the problem by incorporating a new strap onto an existing product. It did not work. He tried to create a waterproof housing for use with existing products, but it leaked. Next he determined he would have to create the product and the strap in order for it to work the way he wanted it to work. But he could only afford to make the "analog" version and produced it inexpensively. It was so "cheap" it was almost a throwaway product. Then after a few years, at the same time that social media trends were exploding worldwide, he raised some money and made a digital version of the product. While not revolutionary, it was functional and sales started to climb. The next version of the product was well designed and introduced some innovative features. Sales continued to grow. The latest version of the product does not resemble the original $30, 35-millimeter-film camera. GoPro had arrived.

Key Takeaway

To move into a marketplace quickly and take advantage of a "market window," create a core product or service that initially solves a problem. Get some sales and iterate your way to innovation as fast as you can. It also helps, from a timing point of view, if your product or service aligns with rapidly growing trends.

CHAPTER TWELVE

BLUE OCEANS
ARE THE DESTINATION

I love using Blue Ocean Strategy in the classroom. I loved using it in my professional life. It's so simple to understand and it forces the students to answer really simple questions regarding a current product or service:

- What can I eliminate?
- What can I reduce?
- What can I raise the bar on?
- What can I create that is new?

You can set sail for a blue ocean all in the hopes of creating a new product or service in a growing marketplace with little initial competition.

Blue Ocean Strategy by Chan Kim and Renee Mauborgne was published in 2005 by Harvard Business School Press. It became a bestseller and still remains popular today. The authors' thesis is

[BLUE OCEAN STRATEGY]

Eliminate	Raise
Which factors can you eliminate that your industry has long competed on? **List those here . . .**	*Which factors should be raised well above the industry's standard?* **List those here . . .**
Reduce	**Create**
Which factors should be reduced well above the industry's standard? **List those here . . .**	*Which factors should be created that the industry has never offered?* **List those here . . .**

that most companies focus on competing against rivals for share in existing markets. Competition intensifies, features blossom, prices decline, and companies lose gross margin and profitability, as competitors rush in to sell cheaper products in order to maintain market share. In this competitively intense ocean, segments are niched and products are commoditized, turning the water red (either the red ink of losses or the blood of flailing competitors—choose your metaphor). So, if you find yourself competing on just price in either a growing or shrinking marketplace, the future is not bright.

The red ocean is simply where every mature industry is today. There are defined competitors, a defined market, and a typical business model in any specific industry. You initially compete on some differentiation and then slowly (or quickly in a rapidly growing marketplace) you start competing on some version of price or cost (e.g., AT&T versus Verizon, Samsung versus LG, etc.). But you can choose to have a mindset that says you *have to innovate* in order to escape a red ocean and head to a blue ocean. How? Companies can choose to avoid this margin-eroding competitive intensity by putting less energy into red oceans and choosing instead to pioneer blue oceans—markets largely untapped by competition. By focusing beyond existing market demands, you can identify unmet needs (i.e., needs beyond lower price or incremental product improvements) and then innovate new solutions that create far more profitable uncontested markets—blue oceans. Here are key elements of a growth mindset regarding a Blue Ocean Strategy perspective:

Focus on current customers versus focus on noncustomers. In most industries there is little effort to attract new buyers to the industry; the focus is on the customers currently purchasing in that industry. With a blue ocean mindset, there is a focus on trying to increase the size of the industry by attracting people who have never purchased in that industry. Think Apple with iTunes allowing *everyone* to buy digital music legally, online.

Compete in existing markets versus create uncontested markets to serve. Sounds good, right? But how do you do that? Existing markets are all the customers doing business in the industry right now, whether they are doing business with you or your competitors. If someone wins a customer, then it is assumed someone will lose a customer. For someone to win, someone must lose. In uncontested markets, there is only a winner—you. No one else is fighting for the business because either they don't know about it or they don't know how. Think Cirque du Soleil in the early days attracting a more adult customer and a higher ticket price.

Beat the competition versus make the competition irrelevant. Competitors become irrelevant because they cannot duplicate the ideas in a way that is a commercial success. Remember, the whole idea of Blue Ocean Strategy is to have *high value* at reasonable cost. If you are doing that, how can anyone compete with you? All the would-be competitors fall by the wayside. An example again is a company like Netflix, which rendered Blockbuster irrelevant due to Netflix's distribution model, first through the mail and then online.

Exploit existing demand versus create and capture new demand. You will be creating value so high that you will be attracting customers who never before would have considered entering the market. Nintendo's Wii appealed to families and seniors by raising the bar and creating a more interactive gaming experience. Yellow Tail wine attracted beer drinkers by eliminating the pretentiousness of wine and making it friendly. Southwest Airlines appealed to business travelers who spent days on the road by creating reduced flight costs for short trips. And the Apple iPad, a keyboard-free wireless tablet computer, gained appeal as a computing device for use by sales and service professionals and even as a next-generation, flat-screen cash register.

WHY DO BLUE OCEANS MATTER?

Blue oceans matter because these markets are potentially large and have less competition, so there is more opportunity for you to grow as the dominant company as long as you continue to innovate. Let's look at a few real examples of companies that created blue oceans for themselves.

Cirque du Soleil, a Canadian company, redefined the dynamics of a declining circus industry in the 1980s. Under conventional strategy analysis, the circus industry was a loser. Star performers had "supplier power" over the company. Alternative forms of entertainment, from sporting events to home entertainment systems, were relatively inexpensive and on the rise. Moreover, animal rights groups were putting increased pressure on circuses for their treatment of animals. Cirque du Soleil eliminated the animals and reduced the importance of individual stars. It created a new form of entertainment that combined dance, music, and athletic skill to appeal to an upscale adult audience that had abandoned the traditional circus.

Let's review exactly what Cirque du Soleil did against the four elements of a Blue Ocean Strategy:

- **Which of the factors that the industry takes for granted should be eliminated?** In the case of Cirque du Soleil that included animals, star performers, and the three separate rings.
- **Which factors should be reduced well below the industry's standard?** Cirque du Soleil reduced much of the danger associated with conventional circuses.
- **Which factors should be raised well above the industry's standard?** Cirque du Soleil increased the uniqueness of the venue by developing its own tents, rather than performing within the confines of existing venues.
- **Which factors should be created that the industry has never offered?** Cirque du Soleil introduced dramatic themes, artistic music and dance, and a more upscale, refined environment.

Cirque du Soleil attracted a new customer, mostly adults as opposed to children, at a high price point, and redefined what a circus is supposed to be. Today, Cirque du Soleil has a valuation of over $2.5 billion.

For the second example, let's look at two current companies competing in the same industry, one seemingly drowning in a red ocean and the other in a blue ocean . . . in the same industry! The Microsoft Surface looks to be a very good product, certainly one that is competitive. It has great specifications, a lot of adaptability, and meets many user needs—and it is available at what appears to be a favorable price when compared with iPads. But it is in a very, very red ocean. The market for inexpensive personal computing devices is filled with a lot of products. Don't forget that before we had tablets we had netbooks: low-cost, scaled-back yet very useful Microsoft-based PCs that can be purchased at prices that are less than half the cost of a Surface. So, the Surface is more than a netbook, but also a lot more expensive.

This is classic red ocean behavior. The market is being fragmented into things that work as PCs, things that work as tablets (meaning they run apps instead of applications), things that deliver the functionality of one or the other but without traditional hardware, and things that are a hybrid of both. And prices are plummeting, with intense competition, multiple suppliers, and eroding margins.

Ouch. The "winners" in this market will undoubtedly generate sales. But will they make decent profits?

Amid this intense competition for sales of tablets and other low-end devices, and notwithstanding sales of its iPad, Apple appears to be completely focused on selling a product that not many people seem to want. At least not yet. Apple has developed and launched the Apple Watch. Apple is saying that it has looked into the future and thinks today's technology is going to move onto our bodies and become more personal: more interactive, more knowledgeable about its owner, and more capable of being helpful without being an interruption. It won't be another variation on the

PC like a tablet, but an entirely new computer experience. Apple's leaders are betting on a vision. Not a market. They could be right. Or they could be wrong. But today, smartwatches are a blue ocean.

I am not bashing Microsoft or lauding Apple. Microsoft thinks in relation to its historical core markets and is engaging in bloody battles to win share. Microsoft looks at existing markets—in this case tablets—and thinks about what it has to do to win sales/share at all costs. Microsoft is a red ocean competitor. Apple, on the other hand, pioneers new markets. Apple's success has not been built on defending historical markets. Rather, it has pioneered new markets that made existing markets obsolete. Its success has never looked obvious. Contrarily, many of its products looked quite underwhelming when launched. Questionable, even. And it has cannibalized its own products as it brought out new ones. Apple avoids red oceans and prefers to develop blue ones.

Which company will be more successful in 2020? Time will tell. But since 2000, Apple has gone from nearly bankrupt to the most valuable publicly traded company in the United States. Since January 1, 2001, Microsoft has gone up 32 percent in value. Apple has risen 8,000 percent.

A Blue Ocean Strategy Exercise

Consider this Blue Ocean Strategy exercise, again using the same brainstorming structure we have before. Imagine you are a student in my Creativity and Innovation class:

> I say, "I just came from a meeting with a group of investors who want to enter the pet industry. Revenues in the industry are now over $70 billion per year and the investors want to introduce a product into the marketplace. But they do not want to be a

'red ocean' competitor. Using the Blue Ocean Strategy, you have about forty-five minutes to solve the problem."

First, the students, in groups of three to four, spend ten minutes analyzing the Blue Ocean Strategy elements.

Next, they spend ten to fifteen minutes identifying possible solutions in each blue ocean quadrant.

Then they spend ten minutes narrowing it down to the best solution(s).

Then they spend ten minutes drawing the Blue Ocean Organic Pet Food grid, which is then presented in front of the class.

So, here is one of the group's solutions for entering the pet industry marketplace: *organic pet food* delivered directly to your home.

- **Which of the factors that the industry takes for granted should be eliminated?** Eliminate the distributors and the retail stores.
- **Which factors should be reduced well below the industry's standard?** Reduce time spent in the store, product filler, and preservative ingredients.
- **Which factors should be raised well above the industry's standard?** Organic pet food made with fresh and natural ingredients including healthy pet vitamins.
- **Which factors should be created that the industry has never offered?** A home delivery pet food subscription-based membership.

U.S. pet food sales are over $25 billion, and one of the fastest-growing pet food categories today is organic pet food. The students examined a competitive industry that is growing and came up with a new type of pet food and delivery service. A blue ocean, for sure. Other companies like Uber, Dollar Shave Club, and Birchbox are all doing the same as they look to compete in their own blue oceans. Fewer competitors, more room to grow, new business models. The Blue Ocean Strategy is a great way to view existing markets/industries and determine where, how, and when you can be disruptive so that you compete on your terms and not the industry's.

CREATIVE / INNOVATIVE INSIGHT

These founders were all professionals in a very large and conservative industry. Clients paid well for their services. Relationships meant everything. So why would these founders set sail for a "blue ocean" and potentially put themselves out of business? Because if they did not, someone else would. They saw the adoption of the Internet and looked to create a new business model for a service that has been around for thousands of years. They completely reimagined their industry's services and, using the blue ocean grid of "eliminate, raise, create, and reduce," they began to redefine their new company's offerings, one where you did not actually need to interact with humans at all. They looked at what the majority of clients wanted in the marketplace, created new "easy to use" streamlined products for greatly reduced fees, and launched the new company in 2001. LegalZoom has never looked back, turning the legal industry on its ear.

Key Takeaway

As you read this, unless you are in an emerging company or industry, you and your company are in a red ocean ultimately competing on price all the way to the bottom. "Change the game and head for a blue ocean" should be a constant refrain in your company. That thought alone will potentially drive creative and innovative thinking.

CHAPTER THIRTEEN

TEMPERO:
THE PARTS ARE GREATER
THAN THE WHOLE

Iteration can play a prominent role in product or service innovation. It's simply looking at the current product and reimagining the "next" version of that product. An MP3 player becomes an iPod. An analog camera becomes a digital camera. But what if you could purposely look to combine the "ingredients" of two or more products to create a whole new third product? This is a brainstorming tool I created called Tempero, the Latin word for *combine.*

When you look at items that have been created in the world by "accident," like 3M Post-it Notes (i.e., sticky notes), the microwave, Super Glue, Teflon, and Velcro, it occurred to me that you could also innovate in a more purposeful way to the same effect. Using Tempero allows the students to "see" current products, break them down, and then try to create a product that solves an existing or emerging problem. Indeed, one of the most important innovations in the world was created by combining elements from two products. Gutenberg arrived at the invention of the printing press by seeing a new connection between two existing products: the wine press and the coin punch.

WHY COMBINATIONS DRIVE INNOVATION

In the ancient world, one of the great discoveries was that by combining two soft metals—copper and tin—you could create a strong alloy: bronze. For the sake of creativity and brainstorming, consider absurd combinations. Take a product and think of an absurd way to make it work. Trevor Baylis is the English inventor who conceived the clockwork radio. What a strange combination! Radios need electricity and the clockwork is a mechanical device. Surely batteries or electricity are better ways to power a radio. However, in the developing world batteries are expensive and electricity is unreliable. Baylis built a reliable radio that people could wind up by hand. It has transformed the availability of information in many of the poorest regions of the world.

Nearly every new idea is a synthesis of other ideas. So a great way to generate ideas is to force combinational possibilities. Get your team together and brainstorm how you could mix your products with those from wildly different sources. Take it to the extreme. How could you combine your key concept with random products, services, places, or personalities? The more bizarre the combination the more original the ideas that are triggered. Vitamins and water? Vitaminwater. I have some rules regarding how I use Tempero as a brainstorming tool:

Combine unlike ideas. Being able to connect and combine nonobvious ideas and objects is essential for innovation and a key part of the creative-thinking process. It allows you to reframe problems. It engages your imagination and thereby unlocks your innovation engine. Essentially, you need to be able to reorganize and rearrange the things you know and the resources you have in order to come up with brand-new ideas.

Talk to people in different industries. Just as Reese's combined two great tastes that taste great together and the tennis shoe met the Rollerblade to become the "roller shoe," look for inspiration in different industries and marketplaces. The cross-pollination of ideas will increase your creativity.

Build on existing ideas. Building on existing ideas and inventions is another way to foster innovation. In fact, when you ask entrepreneurs of all types where they get their inspiration, they can usually list others before them who set the stage for their work. Painters draw on the tools, techniques, and approaches of other artists; musicians build on the styles of other musicians they have heard; writers are influenced by literature they have read; and inventors build on the creations of others. Hollywood uses the idea of Tempero well. Just look at movies like *Under Siege* (*Die Hard* on a submarine) or Speed (*Die Hard* on a bus) or the book *Vertical Run* (*Die Hard* in a . . . skyscraper).

Hire or surround yourself with diverse people. Very innovative companies know how important this type of cross-pollination is to creativity in their businesses, and they make an effort to hire people with unusual skills, knowing that diversity of thinking will certainly influence the development of their products. You need to guarantee that all employees are bright and skilled at their jobs, but are also interested in other unrelated pursuits. Knowing this results in random conversations between employees in the elevator, at lunch, and in the hallways. Shared interests surface, and the web of people becomes even more intertwined. These unplanned conversations often lead to fascinating new ideas. This philosophy is ingrained at a company like Pixar.

PRODUCT INNOVATION NEEDS A MARKETPLACE

You can use Tempero as a brainstorming tool to think differently about possible solutions you have not yet imagined. But you cannot do this in isolation. As I often say to students and the entrepreneurs I mentor, "Ideas are great but marketplaces matter." Every day, it seems, someone on the campus or in the community reaches out to me and asks me if he or she can pitch me his or her idea for a startup company. My response is always the same: Your idea may be great, but what can you tell me about the marketplace? Who is the target segment? How many people is that? How big is the overall marketplace in terms of potential customers and revenue? What are the trends impacting those customers? What is the current competition not doing well? What trends are impacting the marketplace? If you know your customer and marketplace really well, pitch me your idea.

Most entrepreneurs or product developers have it backward: idea, competition, marketplace, customer. How can the customer be last? As an entrepreneur or potential innovator, you need to prioritize your startup or new product thinking this way: idea, customer, marketplace, competition. That is, you come up with the idea, verify its "value" to the customer (by talking to at least 50 to 100 potential customers), size up the marketplace, and understand how to position your product or service relative to the competition. I wish more entrepreneurs and new product development people actually focused on large and existing customer segments, or large marketplaces, because if they do come up with a solution that a customer values, the large market is already there and can fuel them quickly and allow for rapid growth, even in a competitive industry. For example, Facebook did not invent social media (remember Friendster and MySpace?) and Apple did not invent MP3 players (thirty or so companies came before, though they are gone today). Facebook and Apple just leveraged large customer segments and growing marketplaces to quickly iterate or evolve an existing product or service. So, entrepreneurs and innovators, ideas are great but marketplaces matter.

An Innovative Combination Exercise

In class and with local entrepreneurs, I often point out that a current customer base can be used to expand your product offerings or even launch a whole new product or company. For example, if you notice your customers like your pens, would adding a USB storage device to your pen make your customers' lives easier? Would it expand your marketplace?

Stop and ask yourself these questions about your current customer target segments:

- How do your customers use your product(s)?
- Do they use your products with other products?
- What feature or new product attribute would solve another problem?
- What similar products do they purchase?
- What dissimilar products do they purchase?

Again, imagine you are a student in our classroom. Here's your Tempero exercise:

"I just came from a meeting with the head of product development," I say. "She wants us to come up with an innovative product idea that we could sell to existing customers but would solve another existing problem they currently have. You can only choose two products from this chart of nine total products to create the new product idea." I show the class a chart that includes a smartphone, a bike, a Swiss army knife, a microwave, a refrigerator, wireless headphones, etc., then say, "Using the Tempero brainstorming tool, you have about forty-five minutes to solve the problem."

First, the students, in groups of three to four, spend ten minutes analyzing the existing products, choosing two, and breaking them down into their core subcomponents.

Next, they spend ten to fifteen minutes identifying possible solutions based on combining various product ingredients.

Then they spend ten minutes narrowing it down to the best new product idea and the problem that it solves for the customer.

Then they spend ten minutes drawing the actual product, which is then presented in front of the class.

The product ideas they come up with are pretty amazing:

- A mountain bike with GPS security, powered by the pedal power
- A smartwatch that plays music wirelessly and has a 911 GPS panic button
- A smartphone application that lets you "see" what's inside your refrigerator using a remote camera
- Headphones with a built-in hard drive to play music without another device
- A microwave oven that has a toaster built into one side

◆ A smartphone case with four Swiss army–like tools that emerge from the case

Over the last four years of teaching this course, there have been other ideas generated that were so good that they could have been turned into great products, but remember, Tempero is not a product innovation tool. It is a *brainstorming tool* to get your juices flowing inside of a framework structure that might spawn the idea that spawns the idea that spawns the innovative product.

WALK THE AISLES FOR YOUR INSPIRATION

This entrepreneur initially created baby product solutions and then moved into toys and candy—candy through the innovation of a "spinning" lollipop that became hugely successful. The spinning lollipop would actually serve to be the innovative force that would drive the creation of his next product and company. One of the things the entrepreneur believed in is finding and exploiting a gap in an existing market. One of the things he used to do was walk the store aisles looking for disparities or gaps in products being offered. One particular day, he stopped in front of a pretty common household product and noticed a very simple manual version of the product and then a high-end electric version of the product. These products were made by large consumer products companies that should have seen and exploited the gap. But big companies can get stuck on "analysis paralysis," and sometimes they look too long for the perfect answers before they move. He quickly developed his product based on an earlier version of the "spinning" technology and created one of the first battery-operated toothbrushes selling in the $6 price division.

His goal was to get an early product on store shelves and then keep improving it from there. The first iteration of the product was a success right from the beginning, selling as many as 6,000 units a day in grocery stores, drugstores, and large retailers including Walmart and Target. He had taken for granted from the start that the SpinBrush would be copied quickly by other companies. As a result of that planning, he designed the company to work on a short product innovation cycle so it was able to respond very quickly to shifts in the market. As SpinBrush continued to gain market share, his little company began to attract the attention of big players in the market: Procter & Gamble (P&G), Colgate, Johnson & Johnson, to name a few. He was able to negotiate a deal with P&G about licensing the Crest brand for the SpinBrush. It became a huge success for P&G, helping revive the Crest brand, while the entrepreneur and his team pocketed $475 million.

CREATIVE / INNOVATIVE INSIGHT

I met this student entrepreneur at San Diego State University. He was in the business school but supported himself as a freelance photographer, even though family and friends had told him he might not be "good or creative enough" to have a career in photography. All through college, he worked freelance gigs, created calendars for groups on campus, and took graduation photos. Once he graduated from SDSU, he continued with his passion for photography, creating a website portal for teaching people how to take good photos with online video tutorials. He also leased a building, set it up for use by other freelance photographers, and rented out the facilities, which included a "green screen" room. Every time I talked to him, he was learning more about the photography marketplace. He loved photography. One day, during a round of golf, he explained an idea he had for creating a new photography marketplace that would connect customers to potential professional photographers. To be honest, I was not initially crazy about the business model. But I did like the size and growth of the photography marketplace. The entrepreneur teamed up with a partner and together they created a proof-of-concept website portal, pitched it to investors, got some early money in a funding round, and are off and running.

Key Takeaway

However you find your inspiration, you need to qualify and verify it in the marketplace. It's not just about your "gut." It's about "walking the aisles" and looking for gaps in large marketplaces and moving quickly. What "aisles" do you walk?

14

OBSERVATION LAB:
WHAT DO YOU REALLY SEE?

What is the floor made of in an Apple store? What color is it? Millions of people have walked into and on the floor in an Apple store yet cannot answer those two questions. Why? Often, as we move through life, we see but we do not observe. And to be more creative, you must learn to observe what goes on all around you.

I spent eighteen years in a marketing career working with some of the best brands in the world. My curiosity on "observing" instead of reading marketing research reports came about because of my lack of understanding about a Cadillac customer. In my first professional marketing position, I was tasked with managing a large project for the Cadillac Motor Car division of General Motors. I was twenty-seven years old. I knew nothing about Cadillac customers. I knew they were old. Between forty-eight and seventy-five years old. That was about it. So, to become more knowledgeable on the account and to provide real insights, I spent every weekend at Cadillac dealerships for the next year. In addition, I spent time

175

in competitive brand dealerships like Mercedes-Benz and Lincoln. What I learned allowed me to make several recommendations regarding customer service (create and train a new position called service adviser to actually greet and talk to the customer), customer satisfaction (have a clean and warm customer waiting area with newspapers and coffee), and customer assistance (have a technician roadside repair program to help customers as fast as possible). These offerings still exist today (such as OnStar).

IT'S NOT WHAT YOU SEE, IT'S WHAT YOU OBSERVE

Observational research or ethnography or, in plain English, "watching people do stuff" seems to make so much common sense but quite a few people just don't use it. You would think the largest brands in the world would use this every day, but they don't. Certainly, compared to traditional focus groups, mini-groups, or one-on-one interviews, observational research accounts for a pitiably small portion of most research budgets. Yogi Berra's famous line that "you can observe a lot just by watching" is widely acknowledged, but observation remains the most underused qualitative technique in marketing research. One of the reasons seems to be that many clients (and researchers) just don't know how to get value out of simple observation. I have often referred to finding the "customer truth," and in my career I hunted it maniacally. What better "truth" than simply observing what is really happening?

Now, for you to learn how to really observe a customer or an environment, let's go over the key elements of an observation lab, some simple rules that will guide you, and some real observation lab examples.

ASK SIMPLE QUESTIONS TO GET POWERFUL INSIGHTS

The good news about conducting, designing, or implementing an observation lab is that they are inexpensive and easy to do. Anyone with the right mindset can do observational research. First, it's not about what you believe or know. It's not about your opinion. It's about getting answers to specific types of questions. Pretend you are the VP of marketing for Whole Foods, or perhaps a competitor, or maybe even someone on its marketing agency team. We all know this grocery marketplace is becoming more competitive. What could be done differently? What could increase customer satisfaction or sales? How do we boost employee morale? Imagine you are visiting a Whole Foods grocery store in the next few hours. It's a store that you have been in twenty times before. Only this time, for the first time, you go to observe and answer these simple questions:

- What do you see?
- What do you smell?
- What do you hear?
- What are people doing?
- What is the "mood" of the place?
- Who is in the place?
- What is the purpose of the place?
- What color is the floor? The walls?
- What does this place make you "feel"?
- What are you noticing for the first time?
- What is missing?
- Is the place busy? If so, why? If not, why?
- What are the descriptive words you would associate with this place?

For every observation lab, you could have an endless list of questions. Keep the questions simple and limit your questions to fewer than twenty. It's okay if you have an objective in mind, but you need to keep your mind "open" or you will not really observe—you will just see what you want or expect to see. Here is the good news. If you have an open mind you will observe way more than you ever did before. Hopefully, all your senses, not just your eyes, will be engaged.

GUIDELINES FOR CONDUCTING AN OBSERVATION LAB

Learning from watching is, in fact, hard. Since observation skills don't get sharpened in real life the way questioning skills do, you need to train yourself to see, learn, and think when you watch people do what they do. It takes some practice, and some discipline. The one thing I have learned is to look for the ordinary, not the extraordinary.

When you first do an observation lab, you'll think people look like they aren't "doing" anything! They're just going about their business; nothing that they're doing looks surprising. They're walking around at the mall, moving in and out of retail stores, buying their lunch in the food court. They're waiting for their cars to be serviced. Don't become alarmed. Slow down and just start taking real or mental notes about what you see and hear, even if nothing seems out of the ordinary. For example, when my students did an observation lab at the campus bookstore, their first thought was, "What would we really learn?" But they noticed simple things . . . like how people were queuing up in line across a main throughway to get to the main cash register, or how certain products were not offered for sale, or that there was a typo on a merchandising display. And so on. Ultimately they recorded sixty-five observations; then, based on a review, they offered ten recommendations that we forwarded to the bookstore manager. He asked how we came up with five of the recommendations, which he said he would implement. We told him we spent forty-five minutes in the bookstore and just observed.

Here are some simple guidelines that will help you with your own observation lab:

"Ordinary" is what you're there to observe. Don't go looking for something extraordinary. What you're really looking for are the insights hidden in the ordinary. Nothing people do is "natural." You may watch people walking into a retail environment. They'll walk in, look around to get their bearings, walk over to a display or proceed down an aisle, maybe pick up an item or two and compare prices. "Of course," you'll say to yourself, "that's just what I'd do in their shoes. It's just common sense." Observing what they really do is simply the first "truth" about what they really do. That's it.

Whatever you saw could have happened differently. The retail store shoppers could have taken more time, or less time, to get their bearings. They might have gone down a different aisle. They might have picked up more items, or not as many. They might have sought help from an employee. They might have, but they didn't. What they did needs to be explained. Start noticing the regularities: Do most people need a period of time to get their bearings when they come into the store? Where are they when they do this? Where do they look? What do they see there? Is there something about the store environment that makes them do things the way they're doing them? Is the way they're behaving the optimum way you want your customers to behave? Look at the "rule breakers." Who are they? What regularities are they defying? Once you recognize that everything people do is the result of something, you can begin looking for that something. Maybe it's something about them. Or the people they're with. Or the environment they're in. Find the simple something that makes people do what they do.

The obvious should not be overlooked. Take the most obvious thing you've observed. Maybe you were watching people wait to have their cars repaired and they "didn't do anything." Maybe they actually fell asleep in the waiting area. Maybe they spent the whole time looking bored. Maybe they were on their smartphones. Ask yourself why they were so bored—and remember that boredom isn't natural. Humans are the most curious creatures on earth. The service waiting room had a TV, lots of magazines and newspapers, some sales material, and several new-car displays. Why weren't they interested in any of that? Were they interested in anything? Not really; that is, they'd get up, check on the progress of their cars, then sit down again. But maybe that's it: All they were interested in was their cars. They wanted to "see" what was happening with their cars! And that's all they wanted to see. How's that for obvious? What if your dealership had a second-floor waiting room with a full wall of glass showing off the entire repair area? Would being able to see their cars being repaired make people less anxious and more satisfied?

The little details matter. Take good notes. Make short movies. Think about where people walk, stand, sit, and look. For how long. Doing what. With whom. Note every little activity. After "master the obvious," the next most valuable thing you can learn is to "identify the whole activity." Here's an example:

A few years ago we were observing people using a newly designed gasoline pump on a spring day. One of the first "pay at the pump" designs, it allowed drivers to insert a credit or ATM card so they could pay without having to walk to the cashier's station. We noticed a number of motorists driving up to the pump, getting out and looking at it, then climbing back into their cars, apparently searching for something. They'd get back out of the car, go back to the pump, and read the directions—which seemed to present some difficulty. At a certain point we began walking up to people and asked them what they were doing: "Looking for my reading glasses." In the haste to install the new pumps and print some simple directions, little attention was paid to the size and clarity of the typeface for the directions. Since this was something new, the energy company thought providing directions would be helpful. And it would have been, if the directions had been easier to read. Better yet, why not design the pump interface so that it is so simple, you don't need directions.

The "whole activity" is the key. Think of all of the customer's activities as concentric rings of context. Stopping for gas takes place inside the "driving somewhere" ring, which takes place inside the "going home from work" ring, and so forth. Most research projects involve single-activity units like pumping gas, or kitchen cleanup, or visiting a fast-food drive-through; but these aren't generally the whole activity. The whole activity is a set of behaviors that includes these small units plus at least one layer of context. It's "what's going on" from the consumer point of view, and it may be very different from what you think is actually happening. To get clues about a whole activity, look at how people enter the activity you're trying to observe and how they exit. What's going on just before and just afterward? How do they get to the point you're interested in? What and whom do they bring with them? Are they happy, sad, or hurried? How do they leave? What do they take with them and what do they leave behind? If the concentric rings of customer activity are like a big multiring bull's-eye, let the arrow find the target and not the other way around.

The most obvious things are obvious. The problem is that they are obvious in hindsight, and the context doesn't appear until it appears in a real observation. Want to hedge your observation bet? Try watching and talking. My own feeling is that the deepest understanding of people comes from combining an analysis of what people do with an analysis of what people have to say. You can observe people all day long and you will get some insights. But combine observation with engaging with customers and asking them some simple, nonleading questions. Why are you here today? Did you drive by yourself? Which route did you take? What are you shopping for today? Was there something you did not find? I have said it before and I will say it again: "Customers may not always be right but they are never wrong."

CREATIVE / INNOVATIVE INSIGHT

He was just thirsty. All this graduate student wanted was a tasty drink without too much sugar. He worked out quite a bit, played pickup sports, and went for long runs. At the end of his workouts, he just wanted a drink that would replenish him, taste good, but not have artificial ingredients and too much sugar. A drink that was actually healthy. One day in class, after a Pepsi versus Coca-Cola case study, he mentioned to his professor what he wanted in a drink. During the next week, he went to local stores and "observed" all the drinks in the drink aisle. He was amazed at how many drinks there were, with almost all of them having loads of sugar and just not being healthy for you. But he really did not know what kind of drink to create. He spent a fair amount of time talking to others he felt would be potential customers; people who also wanted a healthy natural drink. A few months later, after his professor returned from a trip to India, the professor mentioned what he thought would make an excellent drink. The goal would be to use high-quality organic ingredients and to minimize the use of sugar. Based on marketplace research, they felt that several target segments would want a healthy organic drink as well. After only a few months of concocting the original flavor in his apartment, they pitched the drink to Whole Foods, and the retailer surprised them by ordering 15,000 bottles! The company has never looked back. In 2011, with sales of $71 million, Coca-Cola bought the company, Honest Tea. Kind of ironic.

Key Takeaway

Learning about customers should be a never-ending mantra of someone selling anything to anyone. Observing trends and simply engaging with your customers, or even competitors, can yield the most powerful insights you will ever find. Are you observing your customers? Is your competitor?

15

MARKETPLACES, TRENDS, AND INNOVATORS

By now, hopefully, you understand that by having a growth mindset and the belief that you are indeed creative, you can create or innovate something. But it has to be something the world needs or thinks it needs.

In this final chapter, I would like to leave you with some additional insights to get you started down the path of creativity and/or innovation. It's not about waiting for that great idea that comes to you in a dream or wishing you could create something. It has to do with really examining what already exists—that is, understanding customers, focusing on problems, watching certain trends, studying marketplaces that are evolving, and learning about large target segments (e.g., baby boomers and millennials). Finally, just to get your creative juices flowing, I want to illustrate by explaining exactly how some of today's household-name brands got started. What was their observation or insight that led them down the path of creativity or innovation in creating a successful company? What problem did they solve? Hopefully these insights can help you understand what I have been saying all along: that everyone is creative. It's just a matter of mindset, knowledge, and focus.

IT'S NOT ABOUT IDEAS, IT'S ABOUT PROBLEMS

Before I landed in Silicon Valley in the early 1990s, I used to think ideas were what created companies. Once in the valley, I learned it's not necessarily about ideas; it's about gaps in the marketplace or solving problems that people need solved. A few years back, if you studied ecommerce, would you have seen the "gap" that Etsy (hand-crafted products) filled? If you want to fire your creative juices and perhaps innovate something amazing, study a large marketplace and look at things from a different perspective. Reverse-engineer an existing product or service and what do you see? Can you look at Uber and Airbnb's business models and see what might be coming next? Can you identify a gap or solution to a problem that large target segments like baby boomers and millennials are willing to pay for? Steve Jobs said it best: "You can't connect the dots looking forward; you can only connect them looking backward."

CUSTOMERS MATTER THE MOST

In my eighteen years of marketing, I never expected customers to tell me "exactly" what they wanted or even needed. But I listened for problems that they had. Then, with a careful combination of feedback and testing, along with understanding the customer's mar-ketplace and the current trends, you can design a solution that cus-tomers will buy to solve their problem or meet their need. If you are somehow wrong, customers will let you know pretty simply. They won't buy the product or service. It's not being creative or innovative for the sake of creativity or innovation. Your potential solution has to solve a problem from the customer perspective. Bottom line: Know more about the customers' problems than they do.

DO YOU "SEE" THE TRENDS ALL AROUND YOU?

First, understand that in order to take advantage of a gap in the marketplace or to spot a problem customers are having, you have to understand the current trends that are affecting the marketplace. Are you tracking several of the trends that are occurring right now? Do you even see them? If not, here are the kinds of questions you should be asking yourself:

- Will people continue to shop using their smartphones?
- Will renting things hourly (e.g., cars, services, homes) continue to grow?
- Is eating organic health food going to continue as a preference?
- What other products can leverage GPS technology?
- What else will the fourteen- to eighteen-year-olds consume via social media?
- What's the impact of 2 billion photos being uploaded to the Internet every day?
- Do young people understand and grasp the importance of financial investing?
- What needs to be improved regarding online dating services?
- What fitness trends will evolve and which ones are emerging now?

LARGE TARGET SEGMENTS TO WATCH

If I were looking to creatively solve a problem that could lead to a potentially innovative solution that might launch a major company, I would only be concerned with two target segments: baby boomers and millennials. Baby boomers were born between 1946 and 1964. And these 71 million boomers own about 80 percent of the wealth in the United States and account for more than 40 percent of net household income. In other words, they have the money and they will spend it. Solve their problems and you could do amazingly well.

The second segment will be the largest in the United States by 2025. Millennials, born between 1982 and 1994, will number over 81 million by then. These consumers have several things going for them. Not only are they drivers of innovation (e.g., want everything yesterday, willing to pay for quality), but they will be part of the largest wealth transfer in history from their parents, the baby boomers. So, what do you know about these two segments? What are the trends impacting them? By connecting the dots backward, can you anticipate what they will need next? What are their current or future problems? Creatively "attack" either one of these target segments, solve a problem, and you might have the next great product or service.

THE SPARK THAT CREATES A COMPANY

As humans, we sometimes just lack confidence in achieving our full potential or truly believing in ourselves. How many times have you heard someone say, "I could never do that. I'm just not a leader. I am not creative enough. Me, an entrepreneur?" We have a tendency to place other people who are successful on a pedestal.

Well, having met thousands of entrepreneurs or successful people, I am here to tell you that they are not special. They are like you and me. They just believe in themselves, have a growth mindset, and believe they will have an amazing life.

Just so you really understand how products or services really get created, I am going to share with you exactly how nine products or services got their start. No mystery. No legends. Just some simple facts so that you might believe that you do indeed have it within you to be more creative and innovative in your own life. With that belief in yourself, you just might create something amazing.

Dropbox

The idea for Dropbox was born on a bus to New York. Drew Houston had planned to work during the four-hour ride from Boston but forgot his USB memory stick, leaving him with a laptop and no code to mess with. Frustrated, he immediately started building technology to sync files over the Web. Over the next few months, he worked twenty-hour days to create the code that would allow the technology to work with any computer. Dropbox answered a new, vexing problem for a world where people carry a phone or two, and perhaps a tablet, but have files and photos stuck on multiple PCs, laptops, and mobiles. Along the way, he added a cofounder who had some serious technical smarts, Arash Ferdowsi.

Through a series of network connections, they arranged a meeting with a prominent venture capital (VC) firm. Sequoia's senior partner, Michael Moritz, showed up at Houston and Ferdowsi's apartment. "They were bleary-eyed," recalls Moritz. Pizza boxes climbed the walls and blankets cluttered the corners. He told his partners to do the deal, and Dropbox landed $1.2 million.

"I've seen a variety of companies attacking parts of this problem," says Moritz. "I knew big companies would go after this solution. I was betting that they [the Dropbox founders] would have the intellect and stamina to beat everyone else."

Key Takeaway

Identify a simple but large problem and have the perseverance to solve it.

Netflix

Netflix was founded in Scotts Valley, California, in August 1997 by Reed Hastings and Marc Randolph, both veteran "new technology" entrepreneurs who wanted to rent and sell DVDs over the Internet. Randolph had previously helped start a computer mail-order company called MicroWarehouse and then served as vice president of marketing for Borland International, while one-time math teacher Hastings had founded Pure Software, which he had recently sold for $700 million. Hastings, who supplied the firm's startup cash of $2.5 million, had reportedly hit upon the idea for rental-by-mail when he was forced to pay $40 in fines at a Blockbuster store after returning an overdue videotape of the film *Apollo 13*.

The DVD format had been introduced in the spring of that year and less than a thousand titles were then available. Although the hardware needed to play DVDs was fairly expensive and owned by relatively few Americans, Hastings and Randolph thought the disc had the clear potential to replace bulkier, lower-resolution videotape as the consumer format of choice. They had the previous experience of running a mail-order catalog business and thought it relatively simple to stock and mail DVDs to someone's home. What they were really betting on was the timing of when consumers would adopt the new DVD player technology. And then, hopefully, Internet bandwidth would allow streaming. Well, it worked.

Key Takeaway

Spotting a trend and getting the marketplace timing right is critical.

GoPro

It all started when Nick Woodman, at the age of 22, gave himself until age 30 to make it as an entrepreneur. Four years and one failed business later, he decided to take his savings and go on a five-month surfing trip around Australia and Indonesia for inspiration. But before he even left, Woodman stumbled on what would become the idea behind GoPro. "In preparation for that trip, I had this idea for a wrist camera that I could surf with to document my friends and I on the trip," he said. "The irony was this trip was meant to inspire me for my next business and I had my business idea before I even left." Woodman conceived the idea in 2001 simply as a wrist strap that could tether already existing cameras to surfers. After testing his first makeshift models on that surf trip to Australia and Indonesia, he later realized he would have to manufacture the camera, its housing, and the strap all together. Woodman didn't set out to redefine the market for digital imaging. He just wanted to shoot decent surfing photos.

The interesting question is, how did the consumer electronics business leaders (a market dominated by huge companies such as Sony, Canon, Nikon, and Panasonic) not see the emerging trends of social media photos and video sharing? The industry's leaders were busy trying to stuff more bells, whistles, and megapixels into shiny cameras for the masses. GoPro was focused on creating a "sharing experiences" device. First, it focused on a market niche—surfing and action sports—and now it is for everyone.

Key Takeaway

Initially, problem-solve for a "niche" segment that is part of a big marketplace.

Fitbit

Fitbit got its start after founders James Park and Eric Friedman sold their peer-to-peer photo-sharing company Windup Labs to CNET in 2005. While pondering their next move, Park, a former cross-country runner and avid swimmer, realized two things: that years of startup life had left him in terrible shape, and that he had the resources to come up with a solution. In early 2007, the two men launched their fitness gadget company in San Francisco's financial district, with Park as CEO and Friedman as CTO. They both saw the potential for using sensors in small, wearable devices, but better than that, they saw a huge marketplace of people who wanted to be healthier. They raised $400,000 but soon realized that that wasn't enough, so they did the rounds of potential investors with little more than a circuit board in a wooden box. But the idea was good, and when Fitbit addressed the TechCrunch50 conference in 2008, Park and Friedman hoped to get fifty preorders, although Friedman suspected the actual number would be nearer five. In fact, in one day, they took 2,000 preorders. There was one problem: Neither one of them knew anything about manufacturing. So they spent three months in Asia getting an education in manufacturing and engineering. They solved a myriad of problems and started selling online. The rest is history.

Key Takeaway

Sometimes your problem is someone else's problem; if so, figure out how to make the solution work for everyone.

Nest

The story of the Nest Learning Thermostat begins as most innovations do: with a ticked-off engineer. Former Apple senior vice president Tony Fadell was building a high-end energy-efficient home near Tahoe, California, in 2010 where no expense was spared. The home included cutting-edge technology including solar panels and geothermal heating. However, the best thermostat available was still just a poorly constructed white plastic box. With all of the innovation in home appliances, why hadn't the thermostat kept up?

So what happens when you take the DNA of Apple and design items for the home? How important, creatively, is it to tap into dormant frustrations and solve them? According to Fadell, "Sometimes you look at a problem and think, 'Actually, I don't think we could do better than somebody else.' Then it doesn't make sense. In this case, we knew we could do better. We knew we could innovate.

About 10 million thermostats are sold every year, so it's an enormous market. But there's this kind of higher cause: people can save energy, save money, and we do something good for the environment." Fadell quickly recruited some old friends, including engineer Matt Rogers, to help explore the reinvention of the thermostat. "It started as our frustration and the more we talked to other people, the more we heard their frustration," Rogers says. "That was the tipping point." They designed a prototype, got to a minimum viable product, and started selling. In 2014, Nest was sold to Google for over $3 billion.

Key Takeaway

Take a look at something that people buy a lot of (10 million units a year or more) and see if it can be innovated.

Vitaminwater

J. Darius Bikoff, a self-proclaimed health nut born on September 21, 1961, first conceived of the idea of vitamin-enhanced water in 1996. According to him, he was feeling "run-down" and concerned he was catching a cold, so he took some vitamin C and drank some mineral water. As he consumed the items, he started thinking about the idea of having them together instead of having to take them separately. He founded Energy Brands in May 1996 using his personal savings and contracting with an aquifer in Connecticut for the base water used. He was confident that his water would be successful because he noticed the marketplace was growing for healthier consumer drinks and thought perhaps people would drink less soda and more water.

The individual products carried the glacéau name, with the company's first product being glacéau smartwater. By 2002, glacéau was the top-selling enhanced water brand in the United States, with the company's vitaminwater being its bestselling product. In 2006, the company earned $350 million in revenues. In 2007, Coco-Cola bought the company for $4.2 billion in cash.

Key Takeaway

Sometimes the combination of two products creates something amazing. What could you combine?

Uber

The idea for Uber came to Travis Kalanick when he was trying to find a cab to attend a 2008 LeWeb conference in Paris, but he could not find one. Kalanick cites "Paris" as the inspiration for Uber. At the tech conference, he had a fateful conversation with StumbleUpon founder Garrett Camp. Camp told him about his idea for a luxury car service that was convenient and didn't have to cost $800 for a ride, a price he once paid. Kalanick was in, and the two started UberCab the next year.

As their vision evolved, they changed what was essentially a limousine service into an on-demand cab alternative accessible through a smartphone app. They secured $1.25 million in seed funding and launched as Uber in San Francisco in 2010. In December of that year, Kalanick became CEO. The two vowed then and there to solve the problem with a revolutionary new app. The premise was dead simple: Push a button and get a car. From there, the money came pouring in, including $10 million in funding in February 2011 from Benchmark, which valued Uber at $60 million. "I had this idea of looking at a smartphone as a remote control for real life, and this was the best example I had ever seen," said venture capitalist Matt Cohler.

Key Takeaway

The initial problem can have multiple solutions; be prepared to pivot your creative solution if necessary to address a bigger marketplace.

Chipotle

Be careful of what you prepare and eat—you just might create a company. Chipotle founder Steve Ells attended the Culinary Institute of America in Hyde Park, New York. Afterward, he became a line cook for Jeremiah Tower at Stars in San Francisco. There, Ells observed the popularity of the taquerias and San Francisco burritos in the Mission District. One day, while sitting in a local neighborhood taqueria called Zona Rosa, he watched how the line crew took care of a lot of people in very short order. He took out a napkin and jotted down what he thought the average check was and how many people were going through the line, and he timed it. *Wow,* he thought, *this thing makes a lot of money—it could be a little cash cow that could fund my real restaurant.*

In 1993, Ells took what he learned in San Francisco and opened the first Chipotle in Denver in a former Dolly Madison Ice Cream store near the University of Denver campus, using an $85,000 loan from his father. Ells and his father calculated that the store would need to sell 107 burritos per day to be profitable. After one month, the original restaurant was selling over 1,000 burritos a day. The restaurant quickly gained traction with its fast yet quality food service and began to gain a cult following. Flash forward to 2015. Chipotle did $4.5 billion in sales.

Key Takeaway

Simple observations combined with an expertise could lead to something big. Pay attention.

Airbnb

Shortly after moving to San Francisco in October 2007, Brian Chesky and Joe Gebbia created the initial concept for AirBed & Breakfast during the industrial design conference held by the Industrial Designers Society of America. Their original website offered short-term living quarters, breakfast, and a unique business networking opportunity for attendees who were unable to book a hotel in the saturated market. At the time, roommates Chesky and Gebbia could not afford the rent for their loft in San Francisco. So, they made their living room into a bed-and-breakfast, accommodating three guests on air mattresses and providing a homemade breakfast.

During the company's initial stages, the founders focused on high-profile events where alternative lodging was scarce. The site Airbedandbreakfast.com officially launched on August 11, 2008.

To help fund the site, the founders created special-edition breakfast cereals, with presidential candidates Barack Obama and John McCain as the inspiration for "Obama O's" and "Cap'n McCains." In two months, they sold 800 boxes of cereal at $40 each, which generated more than $30,000 for the company's incubation and attracted Y Combinator's Paul Graham. After its inauguration, the site expanded to include properties in the market between hotels and Couchsurfing. One year later, there were fifteen people working from Chesky and Gebbia's loft apartment on Rausch Street in San Francisco. To make room for employees, Brian Chesky gave up his bedroom and lived through the AirBed & Breakfast service until the company moved into its first office space. Fast-forward seven years and the company is now AirBnb—a household name that has surpassed industry legacy Hilton Hotels in nights booked. As of spring 2014, the platform had 10 million guests and 550,000 properties listed worldwide, along with a $10 billion valuation—making Airbnb worth more than legacy players like Wyndham and Hyatt.

Key Takeaway

Rent something you have or something someone wants . . . then do it again.

SO, HOW DOES IT END?

The people profiled in this chapter were not born to do what they did. They may or may not be special. They may not even consciously think they are very creative or innovative in the artistic sense of the word. But they are. They also believe in themselves. They looked at a problem and figured out how to solve it. So can you. Hopefully, after reading this book and adopting some of the beliefs and tools, you will heighten and sharpen your creativity skills. Let me remind you of the critical elements of being creative and perhaps innovative:

- **A Growth Mindset:** one that believes you should be learning for the rest of your life
- **A Great Environment:** one where leadership and culture fuel creativity
- **An Amazing Habitat:** being in a place where creativity is reflected, rewarded, and demonstrated every day
- **Brainstorming Tools:** sharpen your "creativity" by using these brainstorming tools

You are creative. Believe that and you will hopefully have an amazing career and life. One where you are having so much fun, the lines are blurred between work and play.

INDEX

ABOUT THE AUTHOR

Bernhard Schroeder is the Director of the Lavin Entrepreneurship Center Programs at San Diego State University and he oversees all of the center's undergraduate and graduate experiential programs. He has worked with hundreds of start-ups in San Diego, on and off the campus, is a strategic advisor to several start-ups and is quoted frequently in both local and national media and has spoken at TEDx events. He also teaches several entrepreneurship courses (Creativity and Innovation, Entrepreneurship Fundamentals, Business Model/Plan Development for Entrepreneurs) within the College of Business Administration at San Diego State University. His first book, *Fail Fast or Win Big* was released in February 2015.

Since moving to San Diego in 1997, he specialized in working with founders and venture capitalists in either growth or turnaround opportunities with several companies ranging from $10 million to $150 million. Bernhard brings over 20 years of branding, marketing, and entrepreneurial experience both as a Senior Partner in a global integrated marketing agency and as a former Chief Marketing Officer on the client side.

Prior to moving to San Diego, Bernhard was a Senior Partner in the worlds' largest integrated marketing communications agency, CKS Partners, which in 1998 had offices in over 30 countries, more than 10,000 employees and over $1 billion in revenue. He joined CKS in 1991 when the firm had only 21 employees and just $2.5 million in revenue. He opened the first out of state agency office for CKS in 1993 in Portland Oregon and, working with the other four partners, grew the firm to almost $40 million in revenue by 1995 and led CKS to a successful initial public offering that same year. Today, he mentors about 20 startup founders that are located in San Diego, San Francisco, California and Austin, Texas.